JUDY FAWCETT'S
DAMSELS IN DISTRESS COLORING BOOK

DE-STRESS WHILE COLORING MY DAMSELS IN DISTRESS

© COPYRIGHT 2020 JUDY FAWCETT

ALL RIGHTS RESERVED

ALL CHARACTERS HEREIN HAVE BEEN CREATED BY JUDY FAWCETT AND APPEAR IN HER BOOKS. ANY RE-CREATION OR PROPAGATION OF THE PAGES HEREIN IS PROHIBITED, EXCEPT FOR BRIEF QUOTATIONS IN REVIEWS.

CARISSA BEING AUCTIONED • IN THE DUDE RANCH CAPER
BOOK COVER

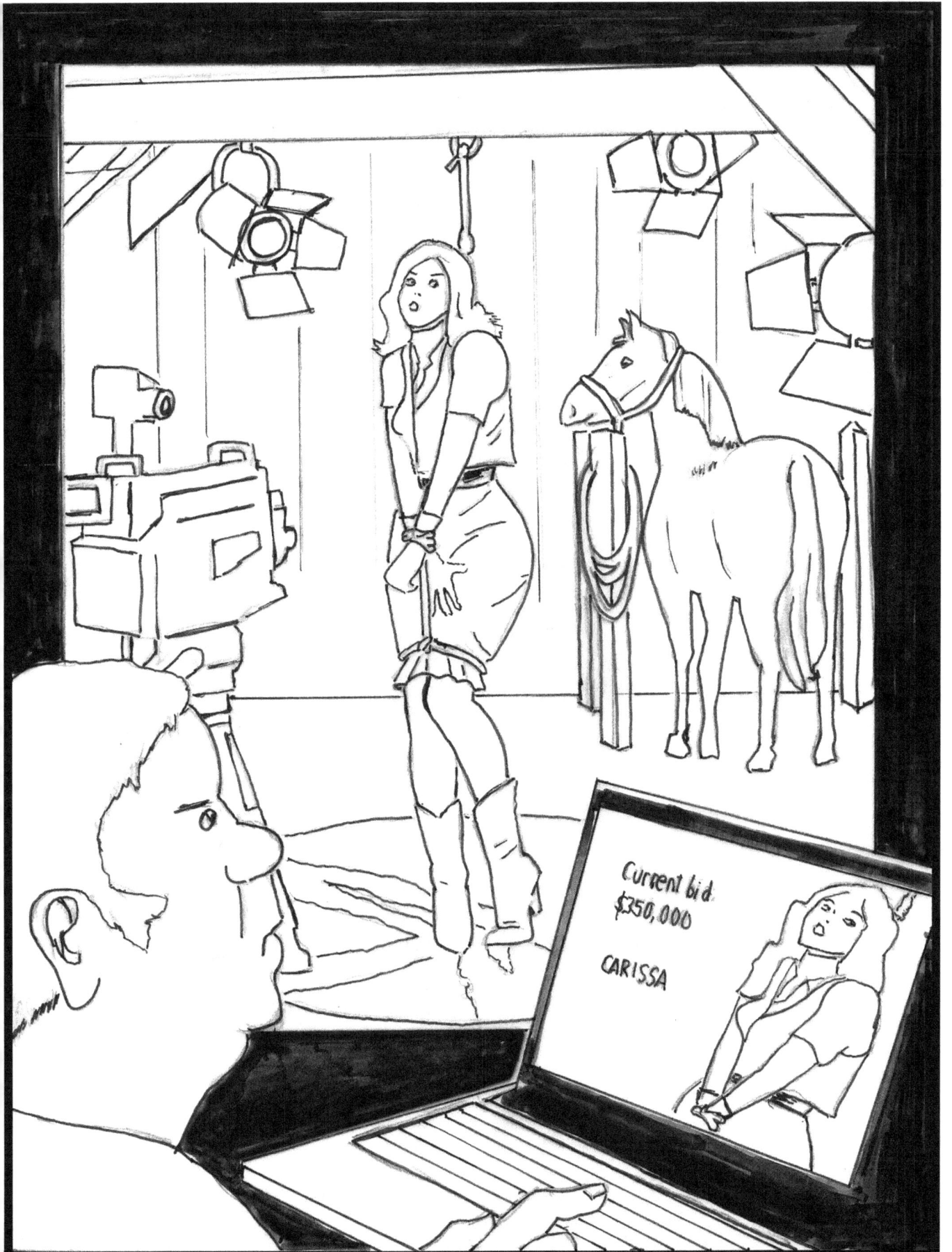

PARTY GIRL INSIDE VAN • IN THE GIRLS COLLEGE CAPER

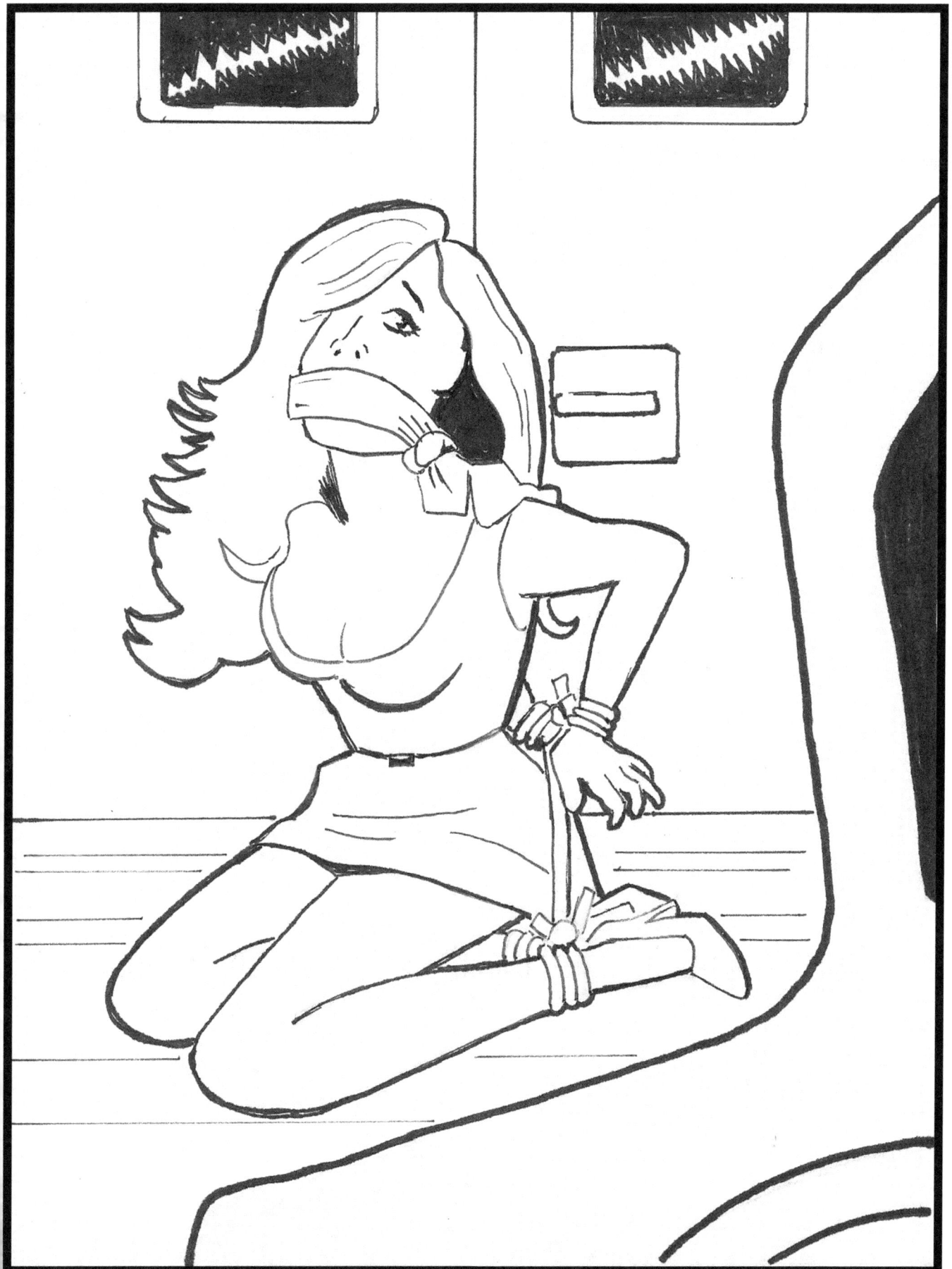

FAITH ANN TIED UP IN THE LIBRARY • IN THE HAUNTED MANSION

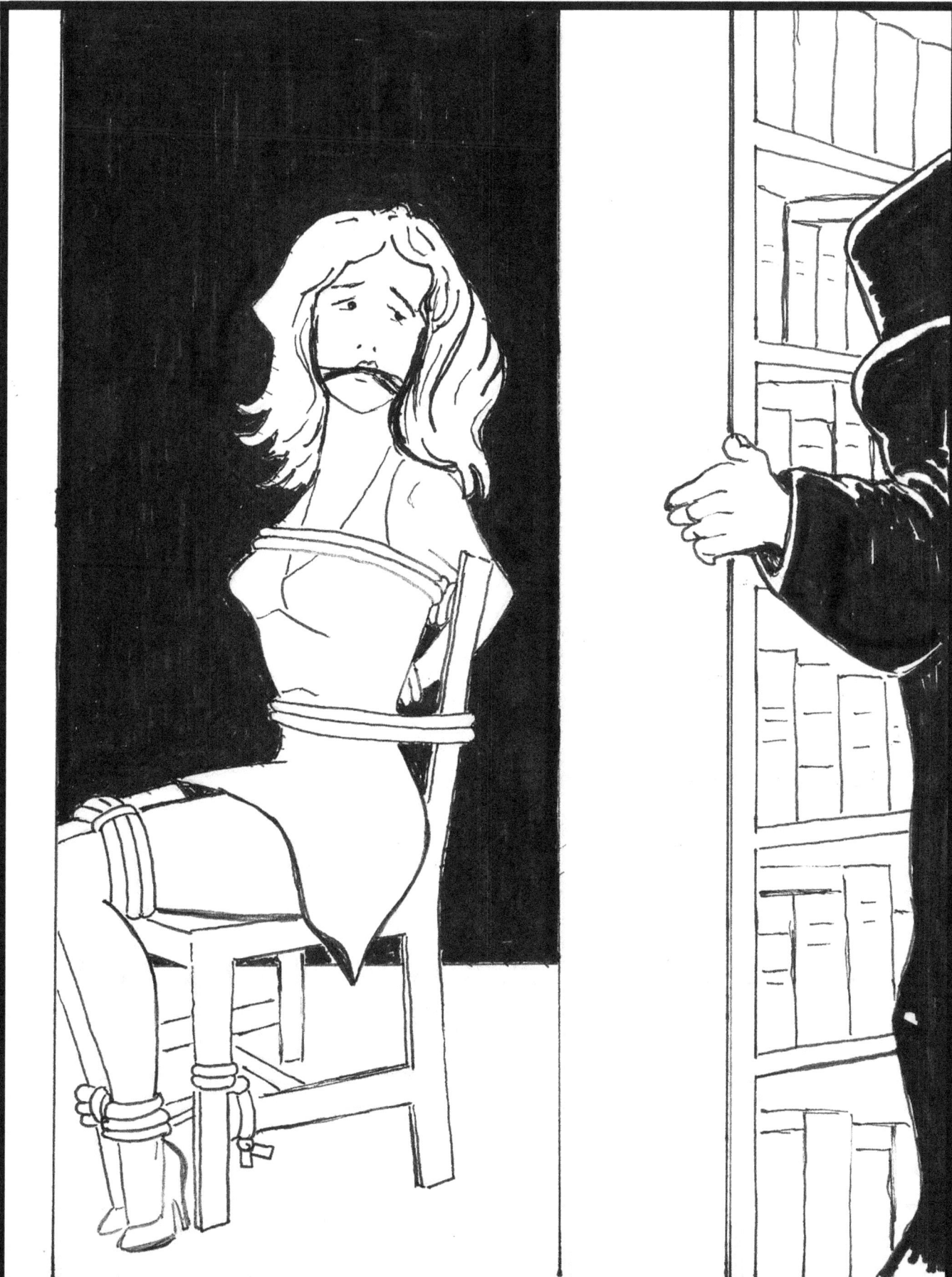

DAPHNE TIED UP IN THE TRUNK OF A CAR • IN THE ROCKABILLY CAPER BOOK COVER

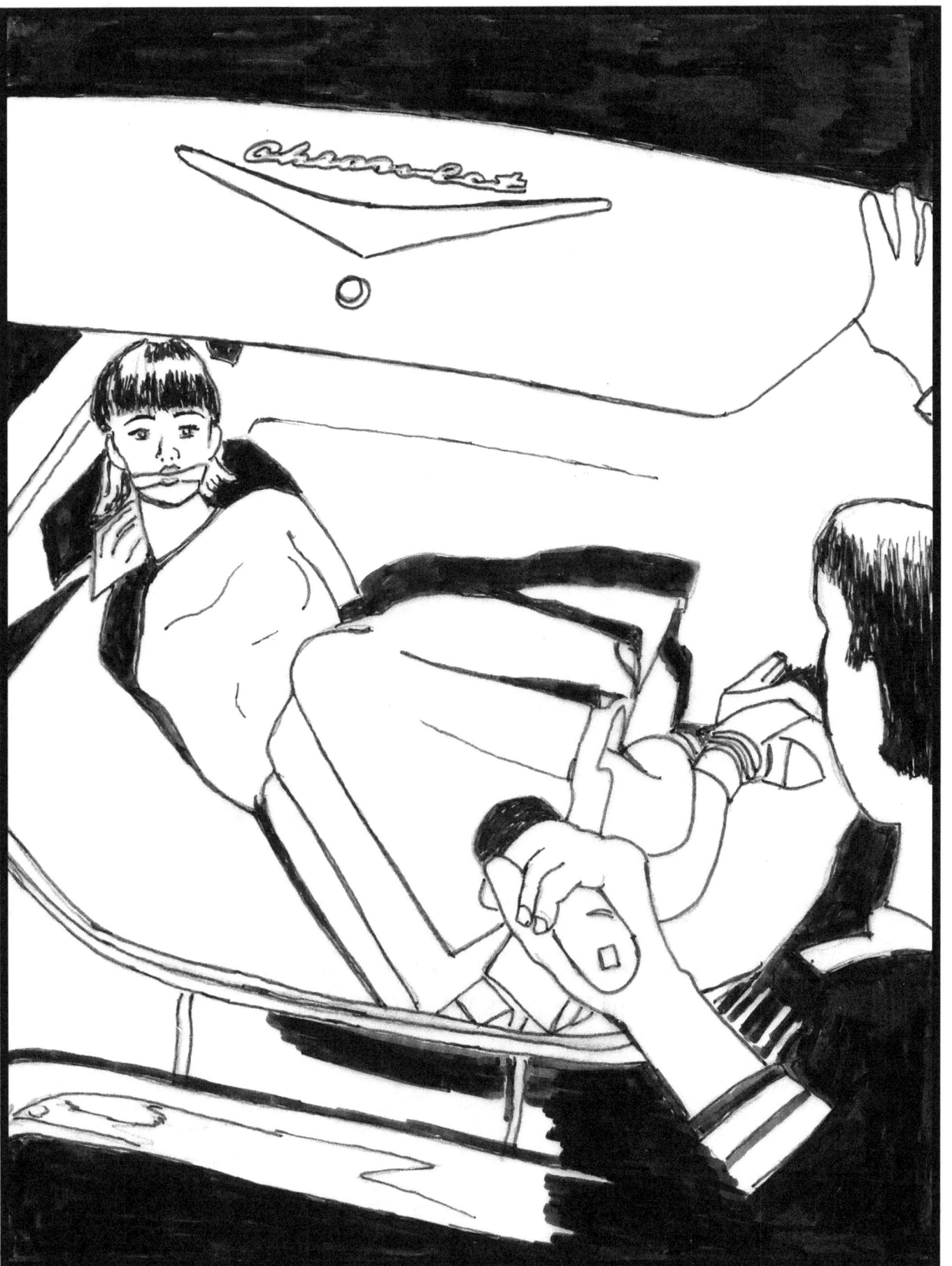

DAPHNE & HEATHER TIED UP IN THE CABIN BASEMENT
IN THE ROCKABILLY CAPER

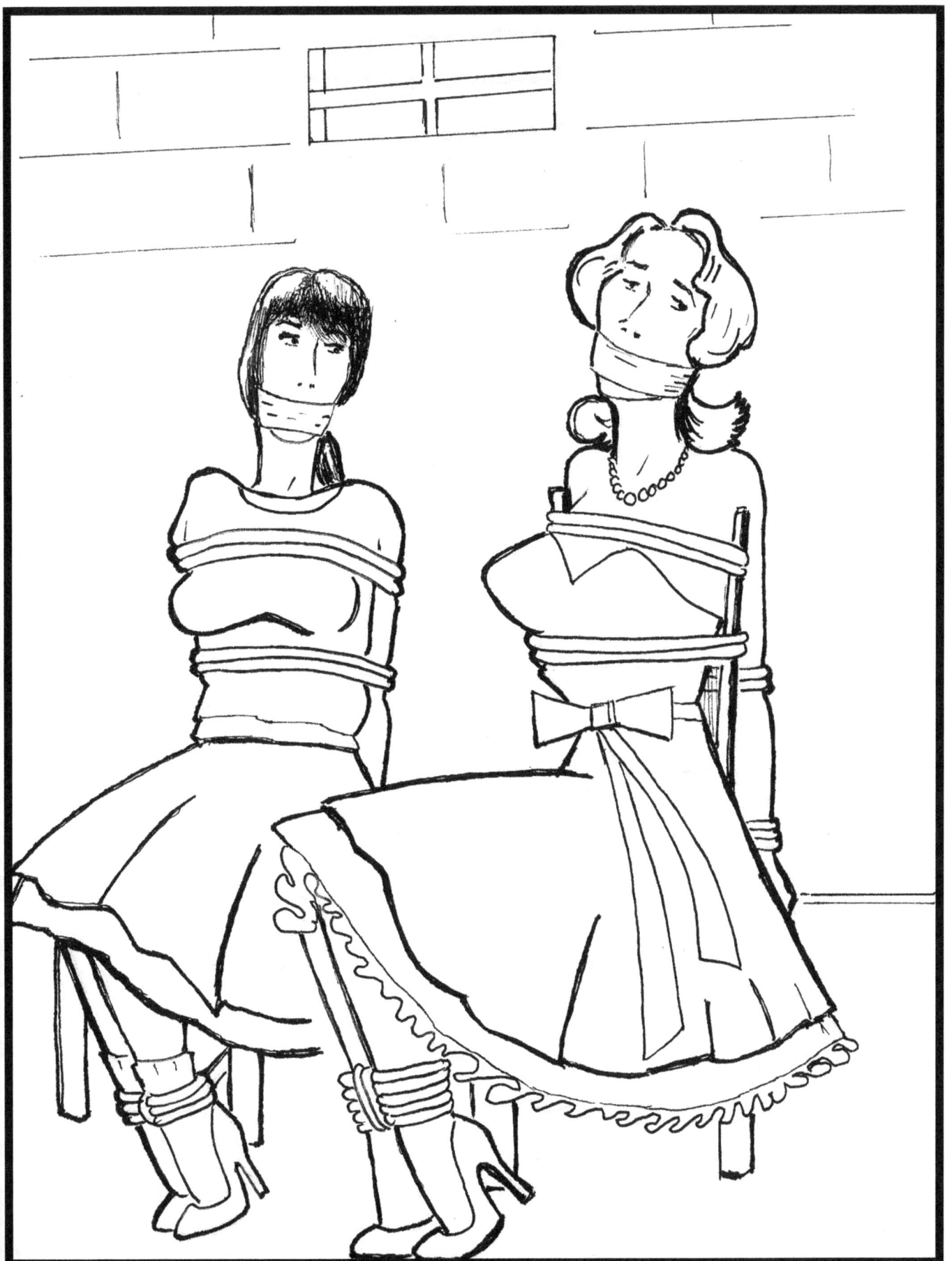

GIRL WALKING THE PLANK • IN THE LIGHTHOUSE CAPER
BOOK COVER

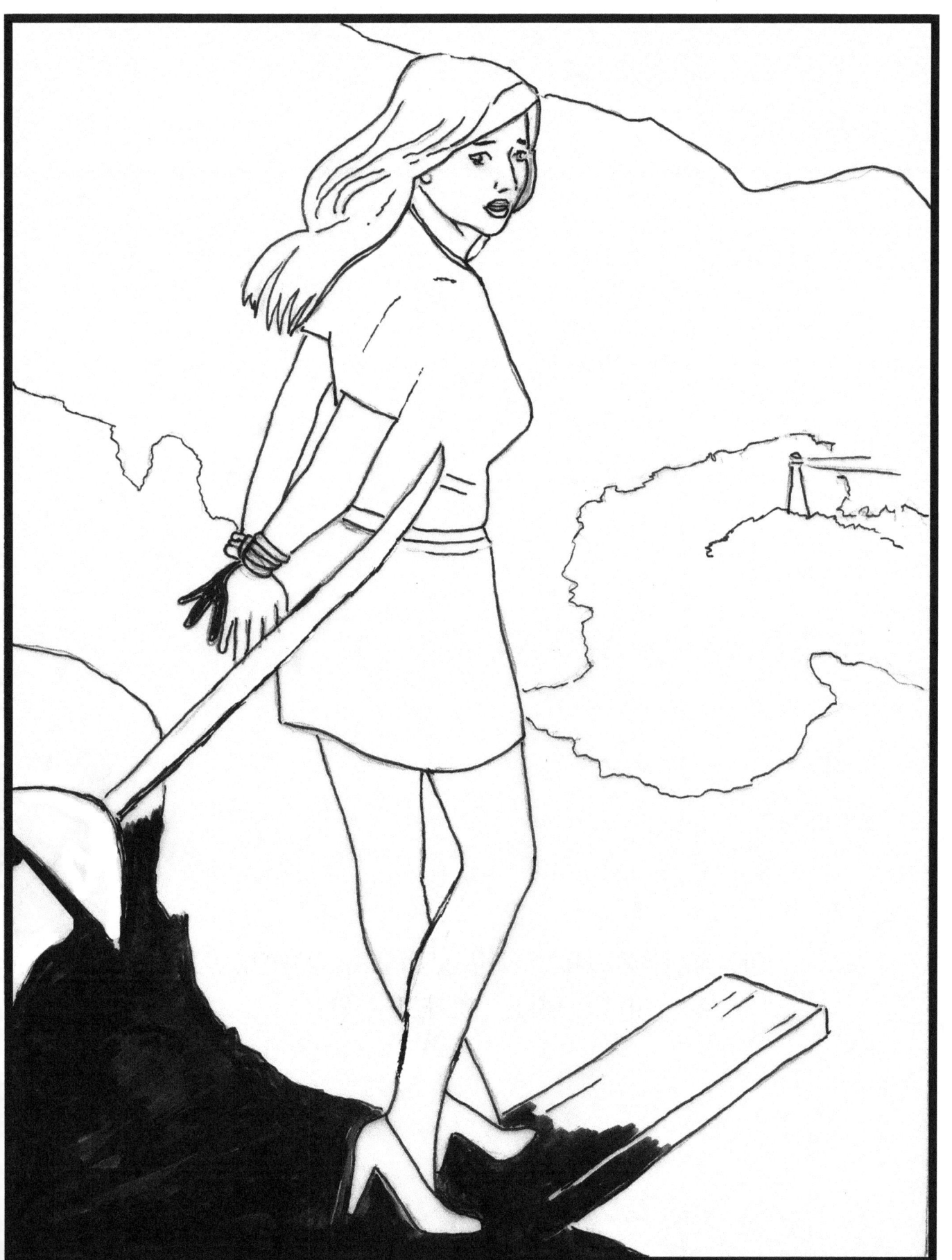

TIFFANY, HEATHER & BETHANY TIED UP IN THEIR VAN
IN THE GIRLS COLLEGE CAPER

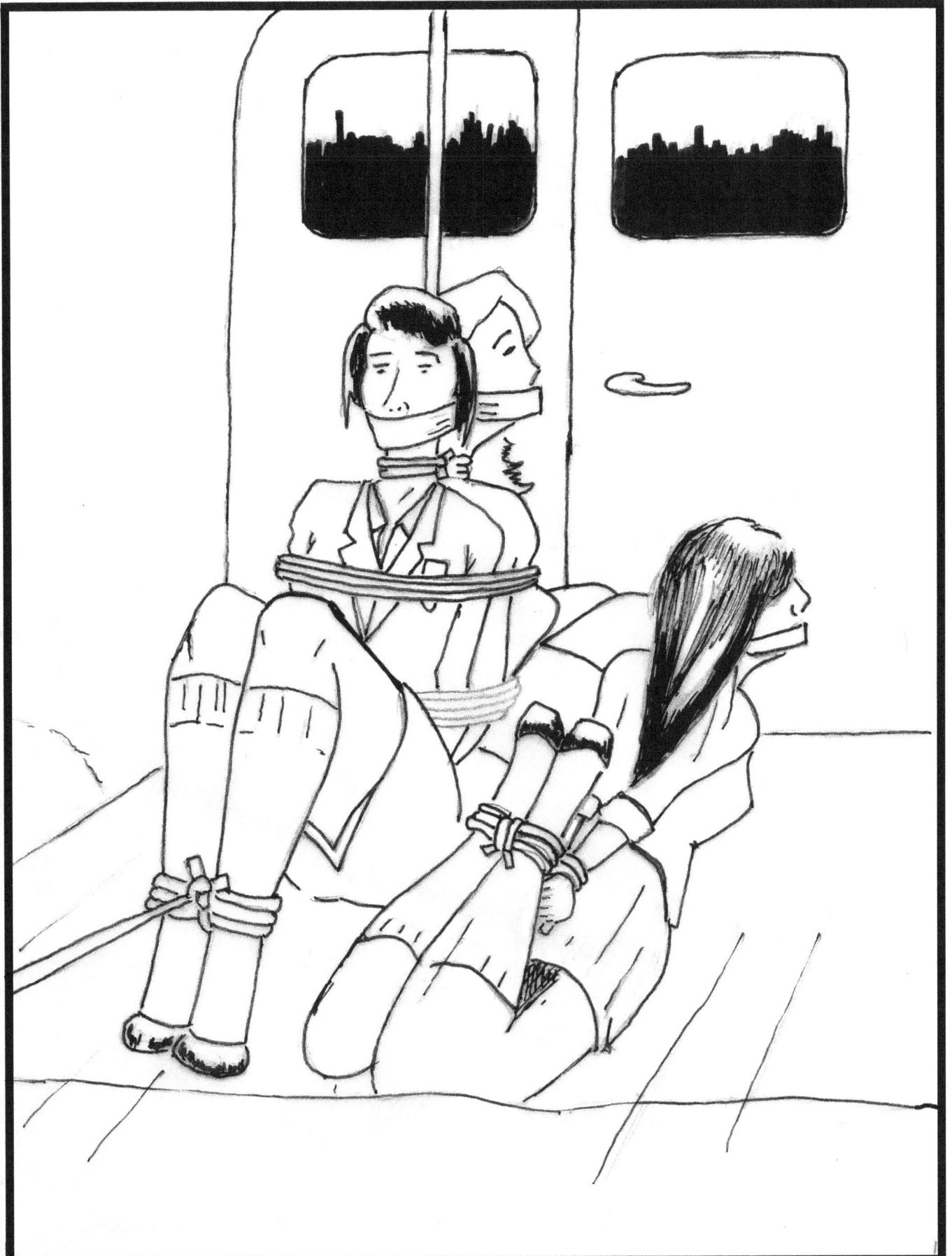

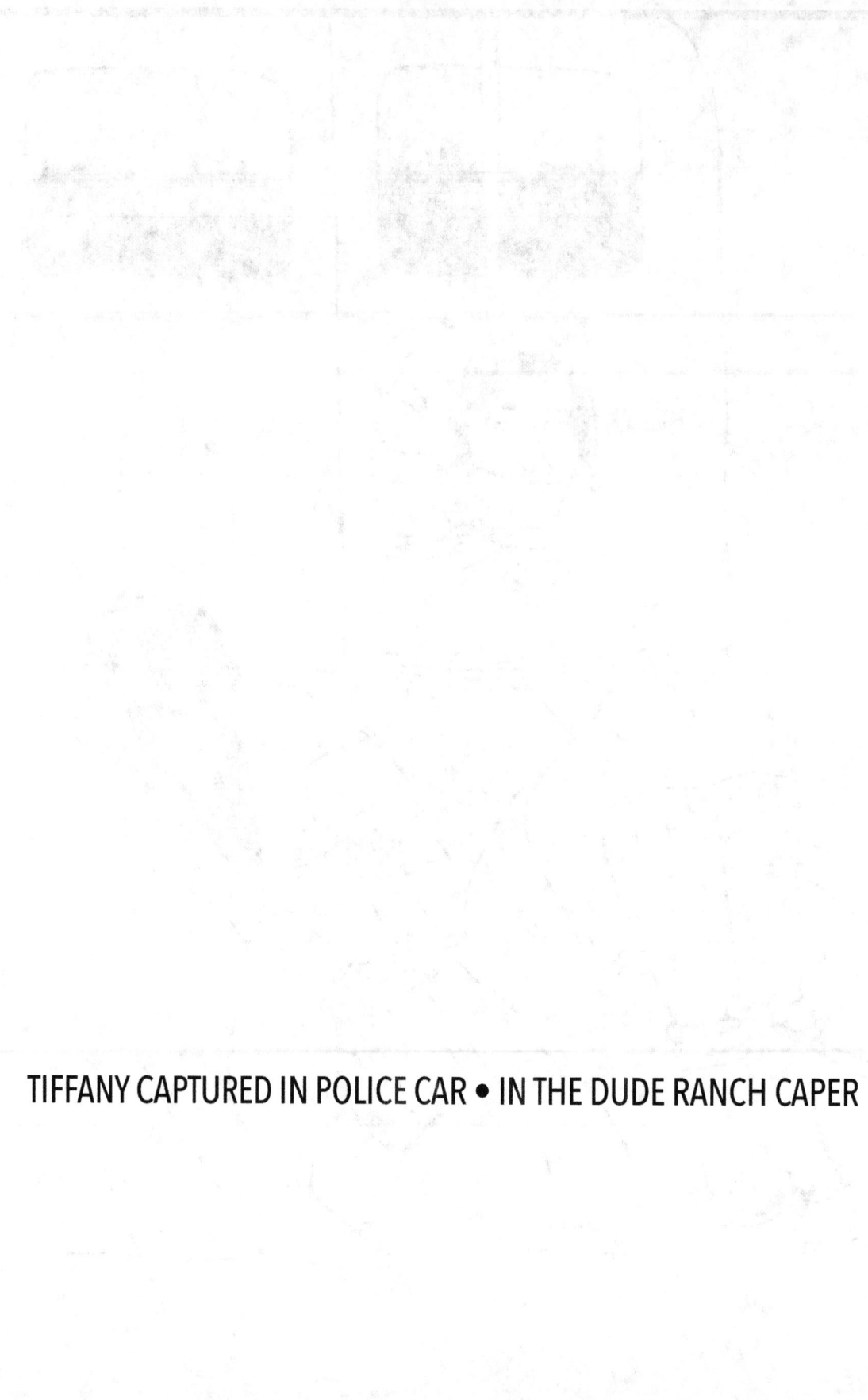

TIFFANY CAPTURED IN POLICE CAR • IN THE DUDE RANCH CAPER

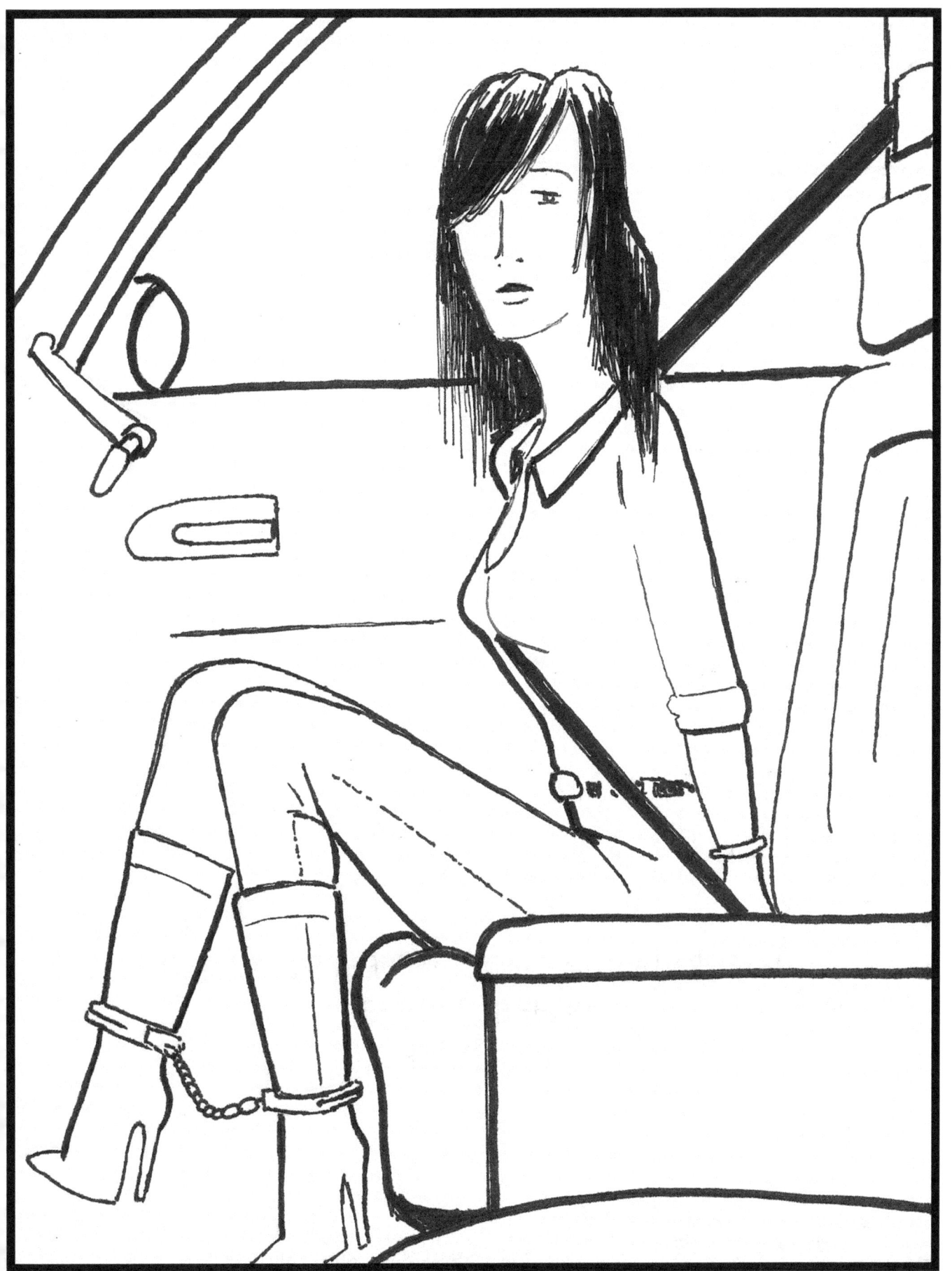

HEATHER & FAITH ANN TIED UP IN THE HOTEL BASEMENT
IN THE HOTEL CAPER
BOOK COVER

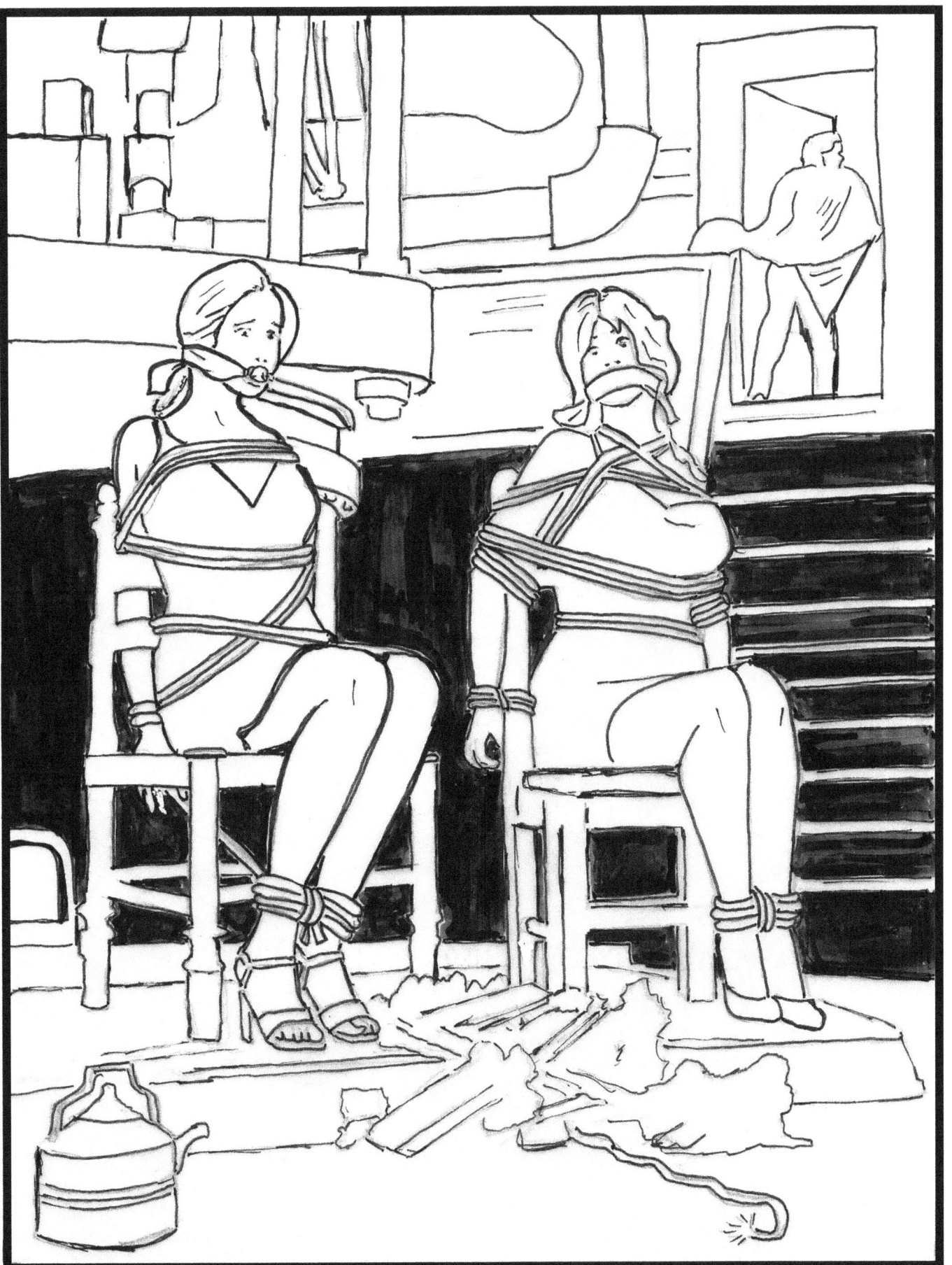

ANASTASIA LANE, CUFFED TO HER BED • IN THE HOTEL CAPER

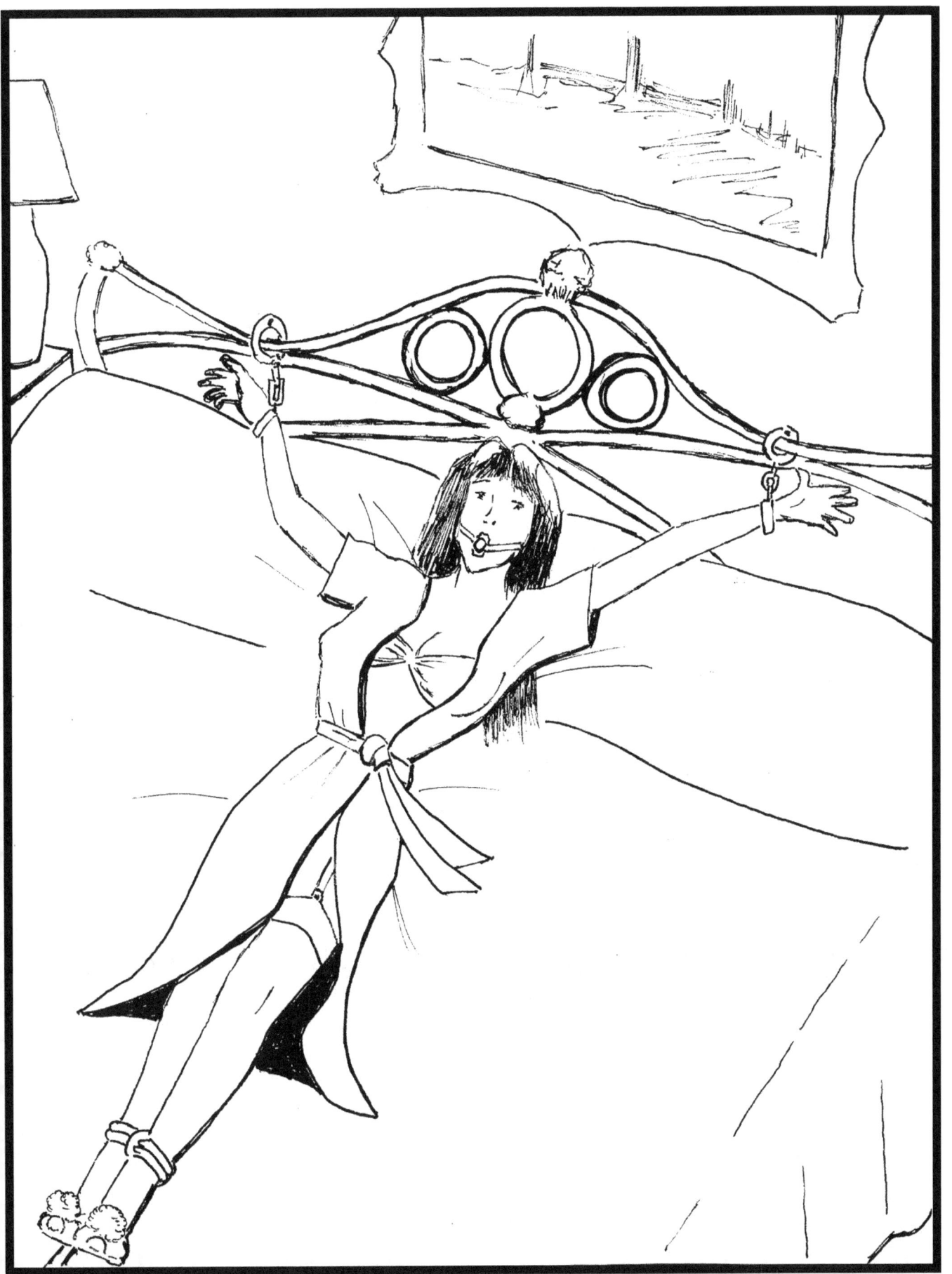

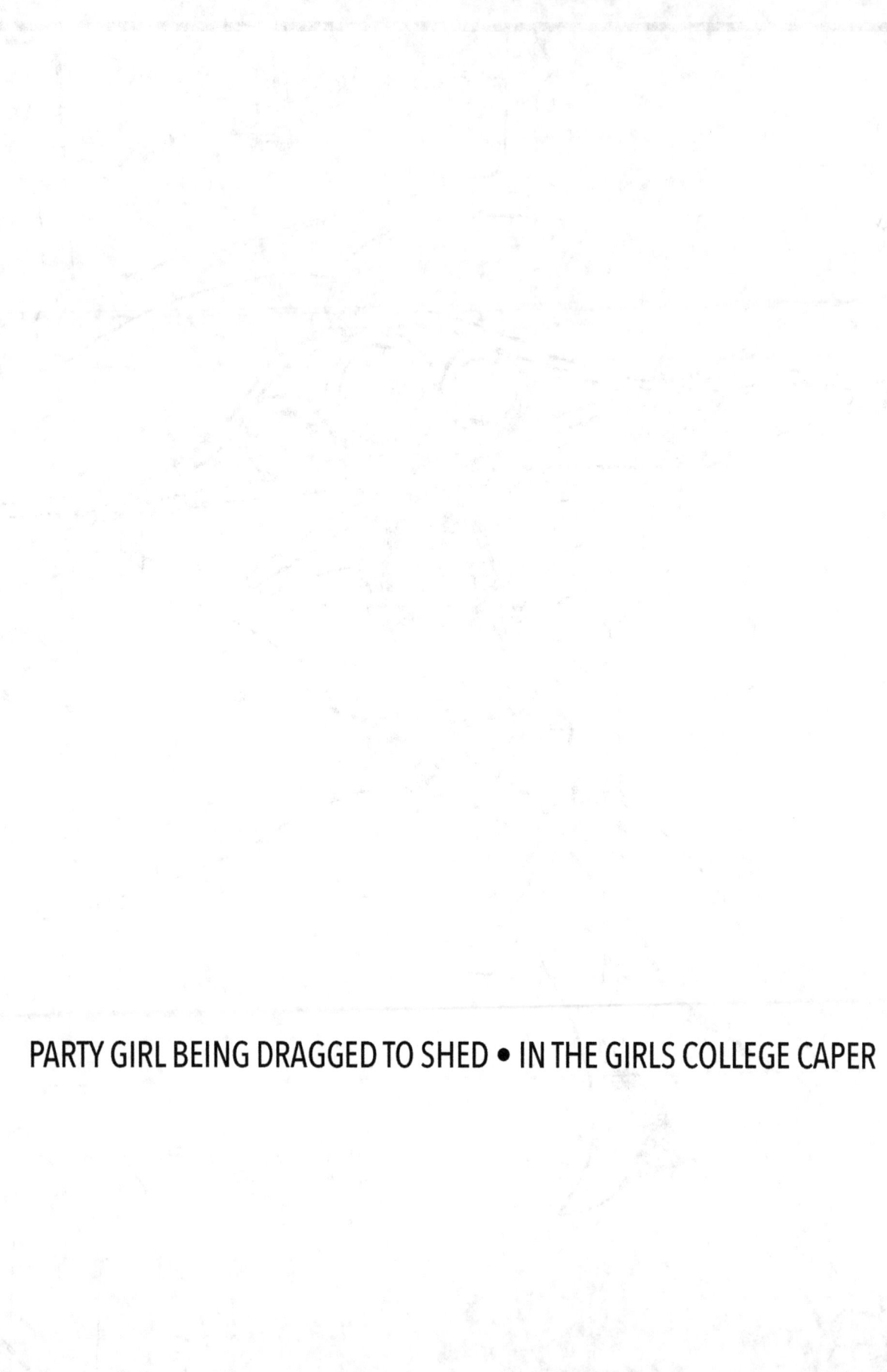
PARTY GIRL BEING DRAGGED TO SHED • IN THE GIRLS COLLEGE CAPER

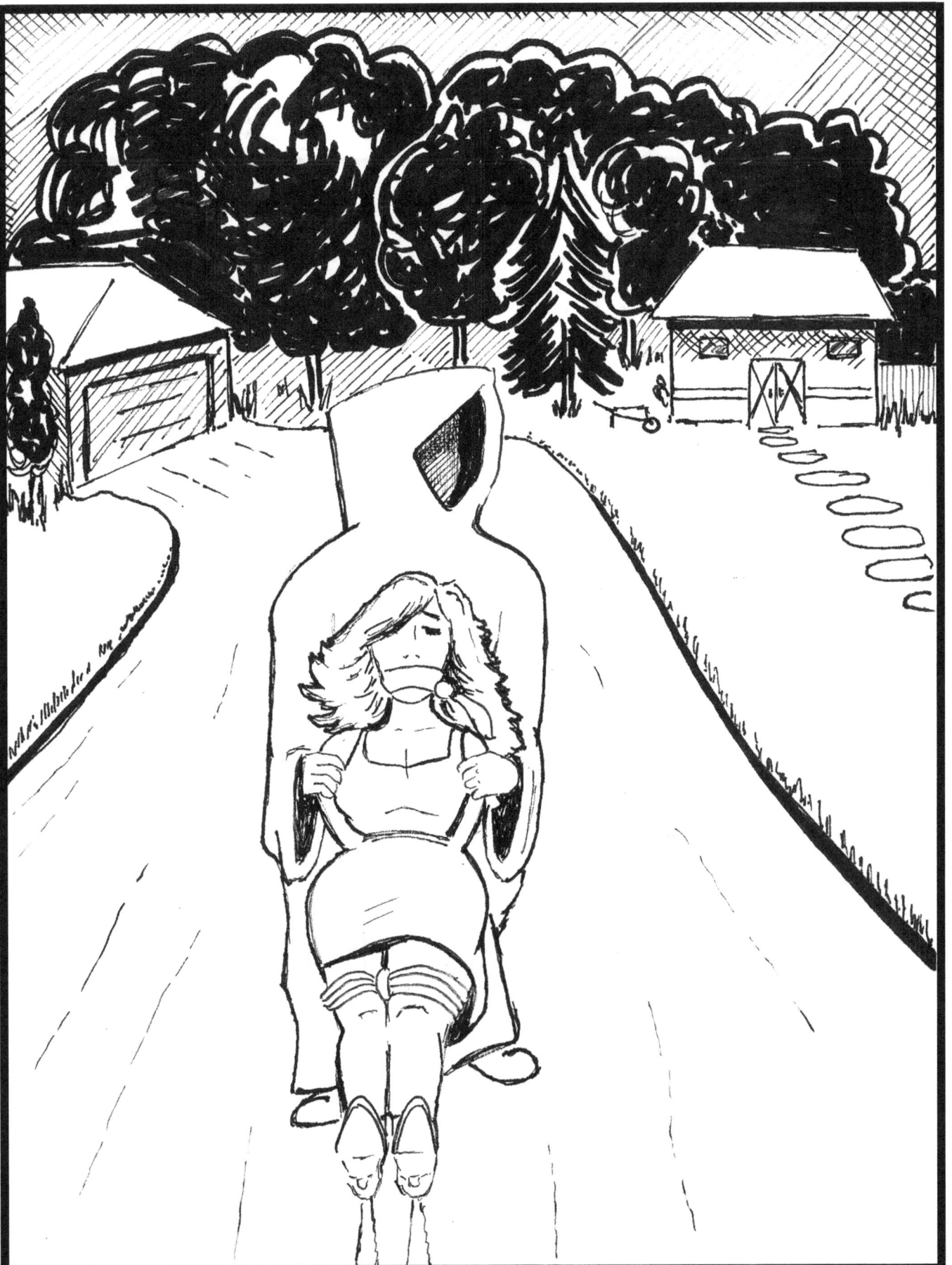

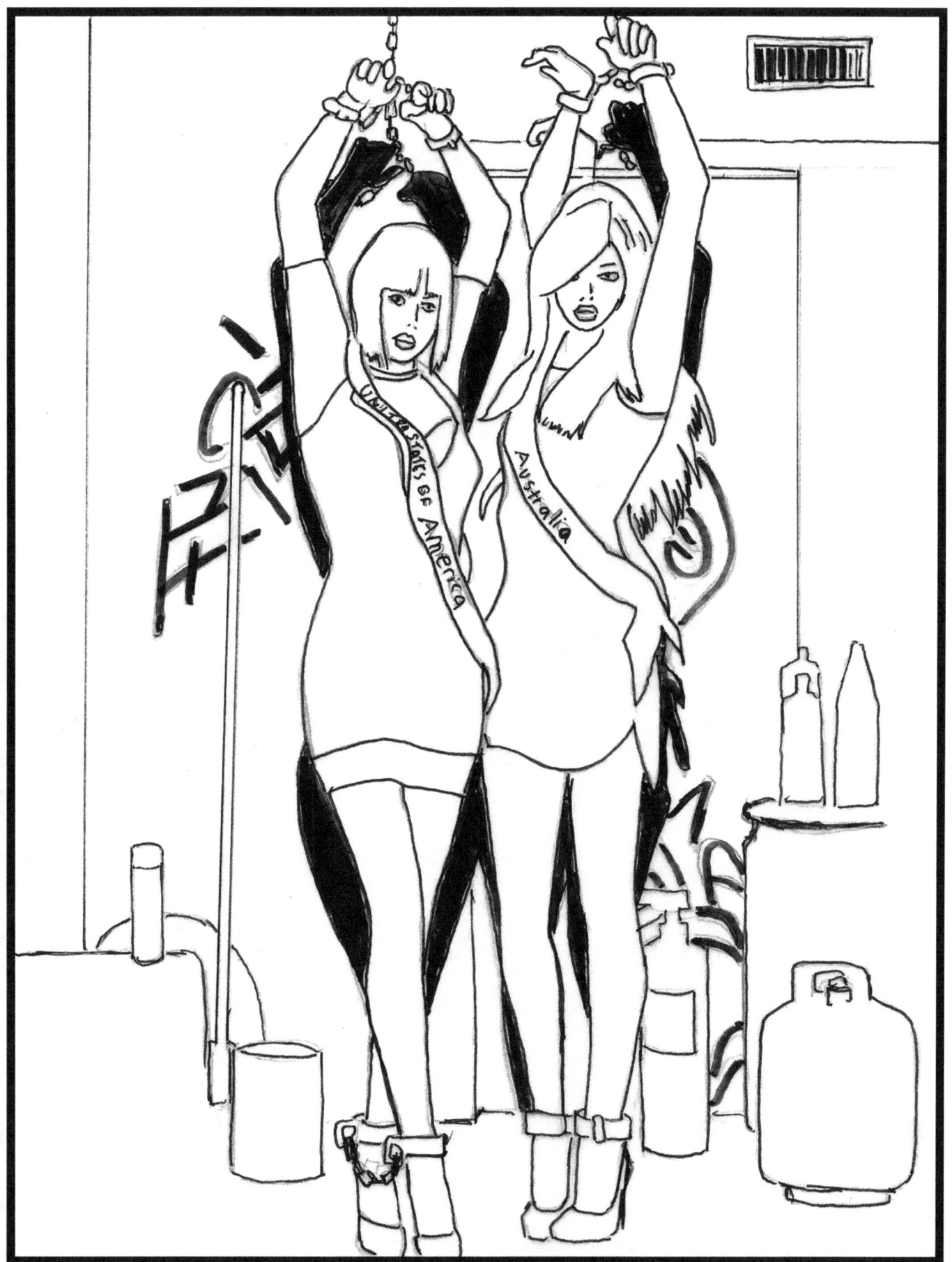

PARTY GIRL TIED UP IN SHED • IN THE GIRLS COLLEGE CAPER

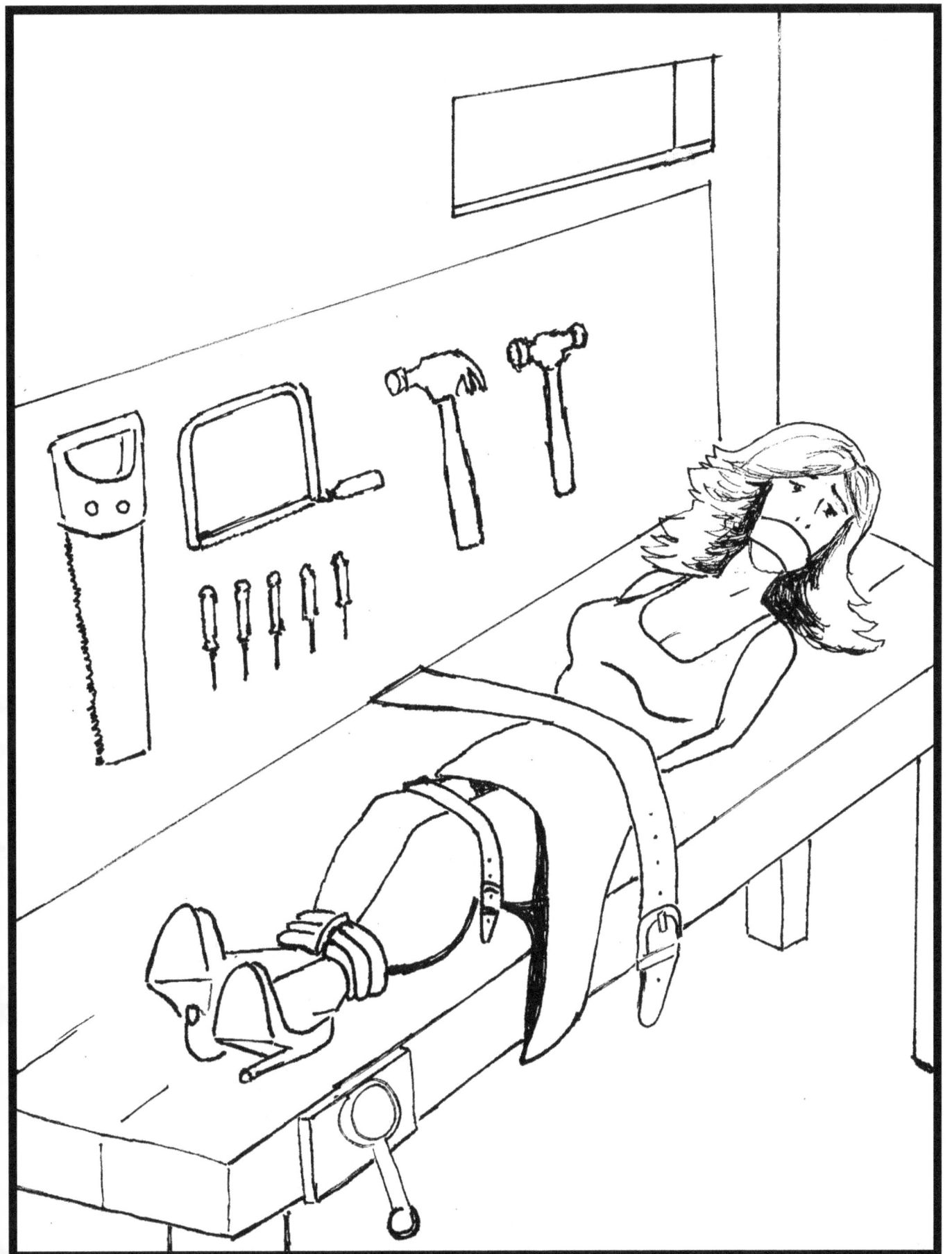

TIFFANY, HEATHER, FAITH ANN & BETHANY ADMIRING THEMSELVES
IN THE GIRLS COLLEGE CAPER

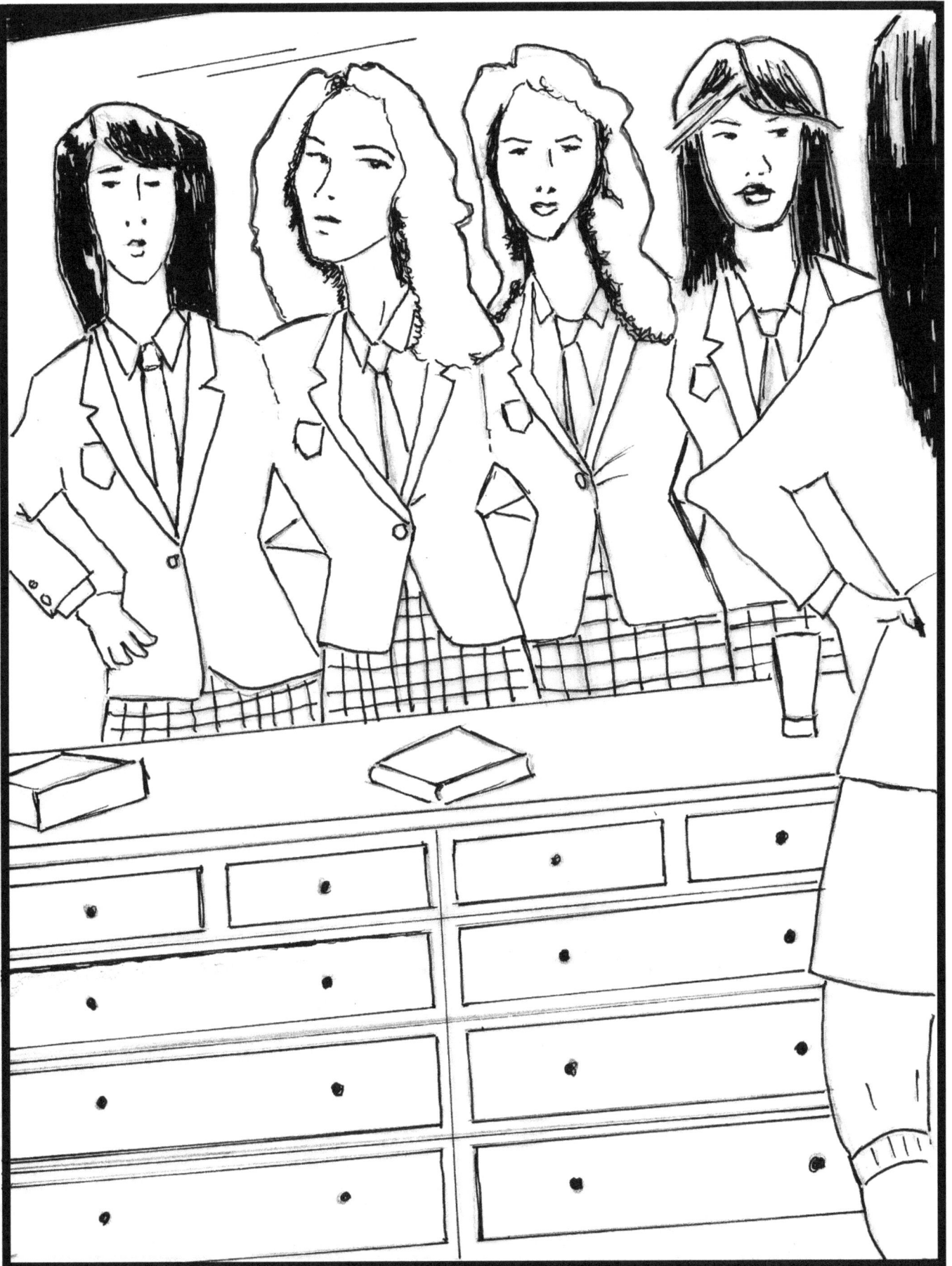

TIFFANY BEING PREPARED TO BE BOILED TO DEATH
IN THE MOVIE STUDIO CAPER
BOOK COVER

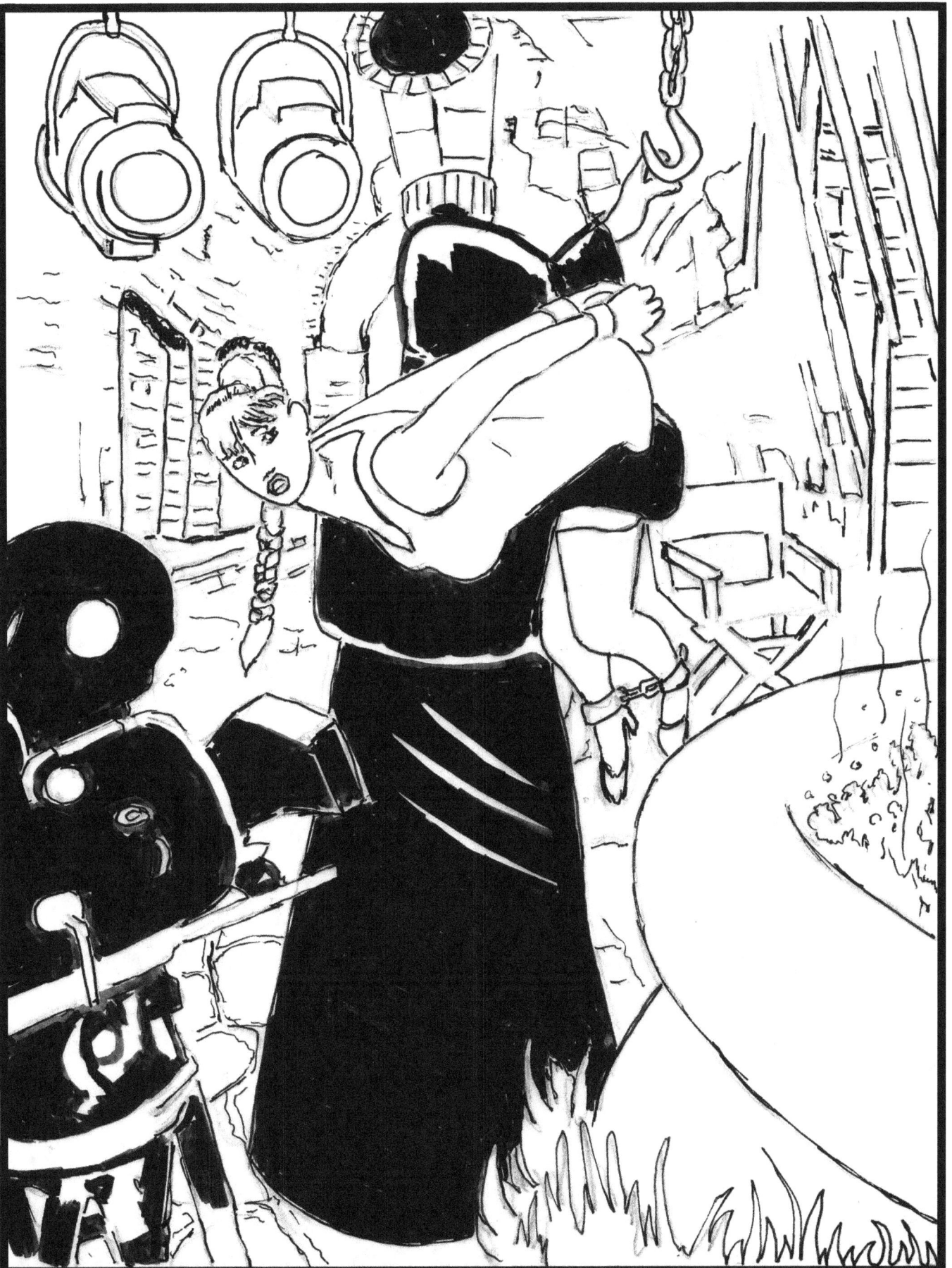

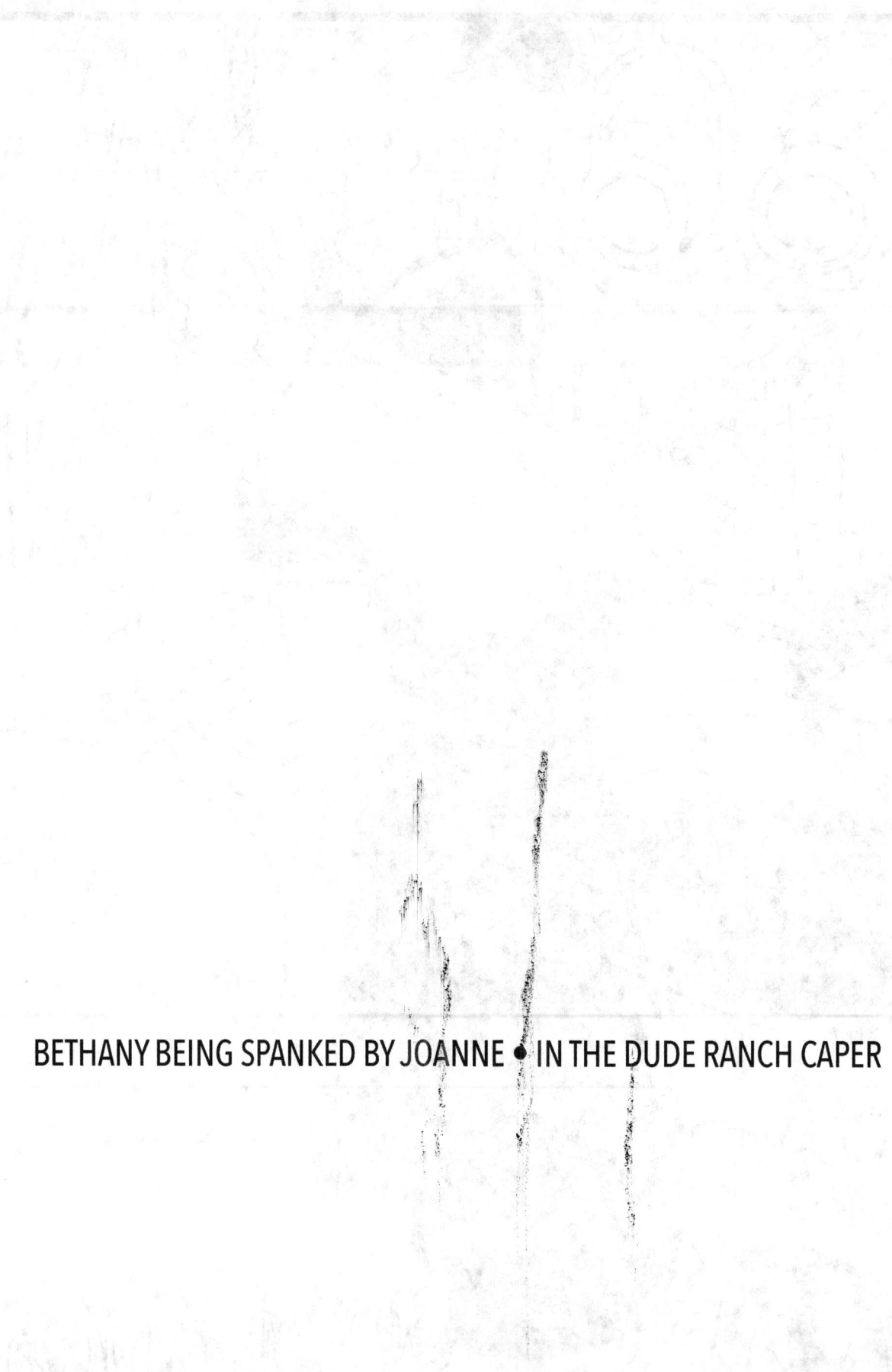

BETHANY BEING SPANKED BY JOANNE • IN THE DUDE RANCH CAPER

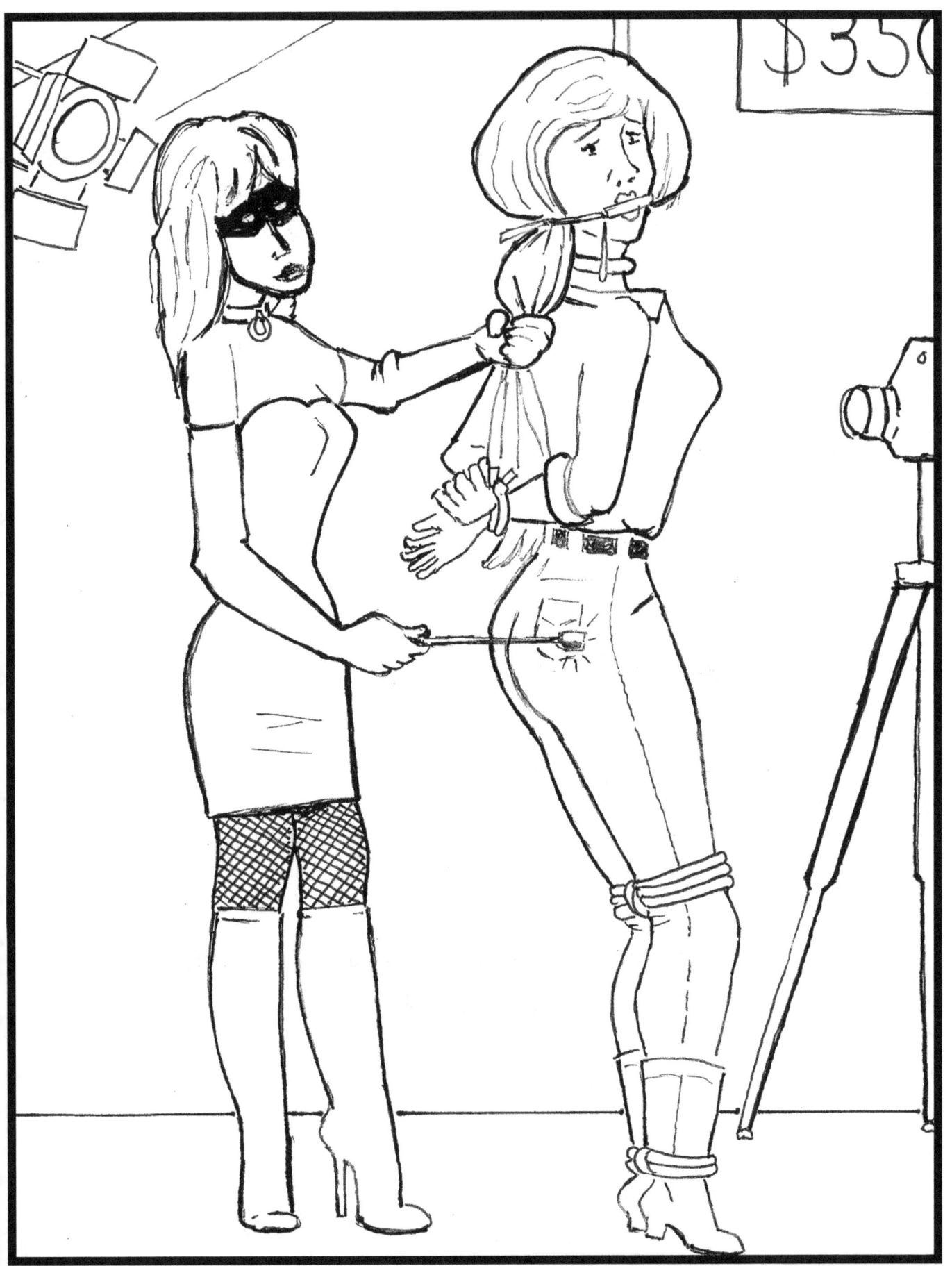

THE GIRLS IN DANGER • IN THE HAUNTED MANSION
BOOK COVER

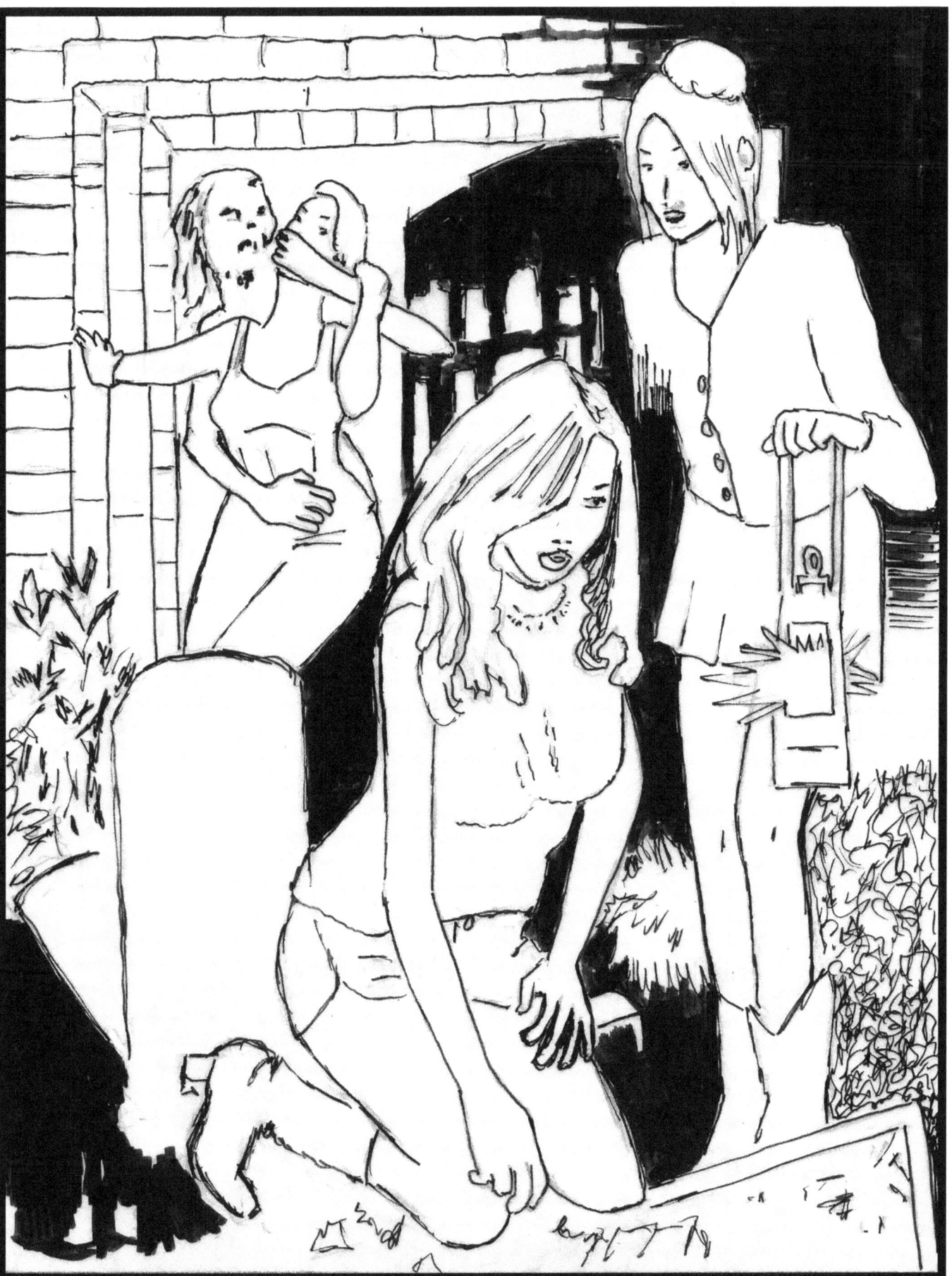

HEATHER IN CAVE • IN THE LIGHTHOUSE CAPER

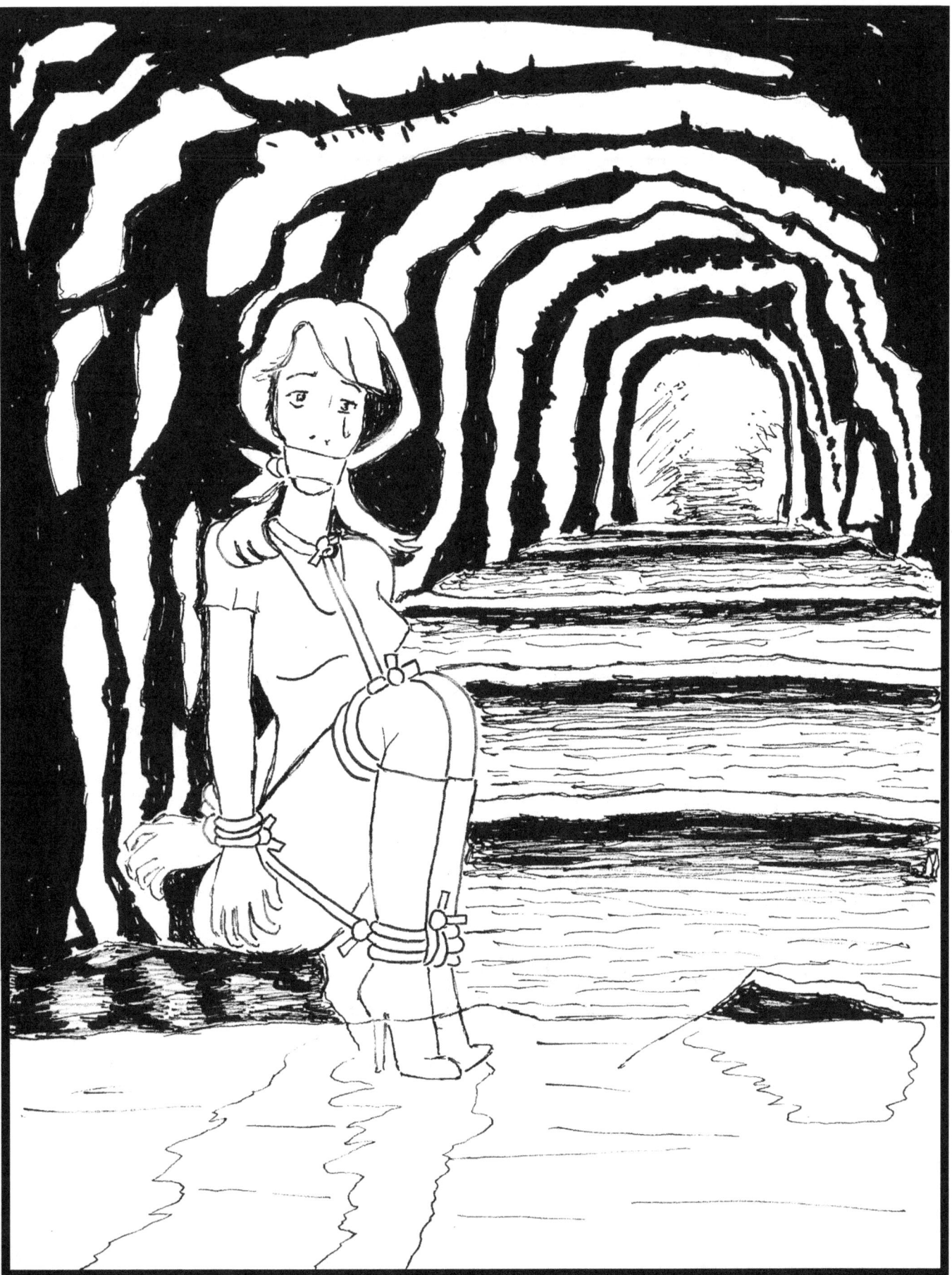

FAITH ANN, HEATHER, BETHANY & TIFFANY UP FOR AUCTION
IN THE DUDE RANCH CAPER

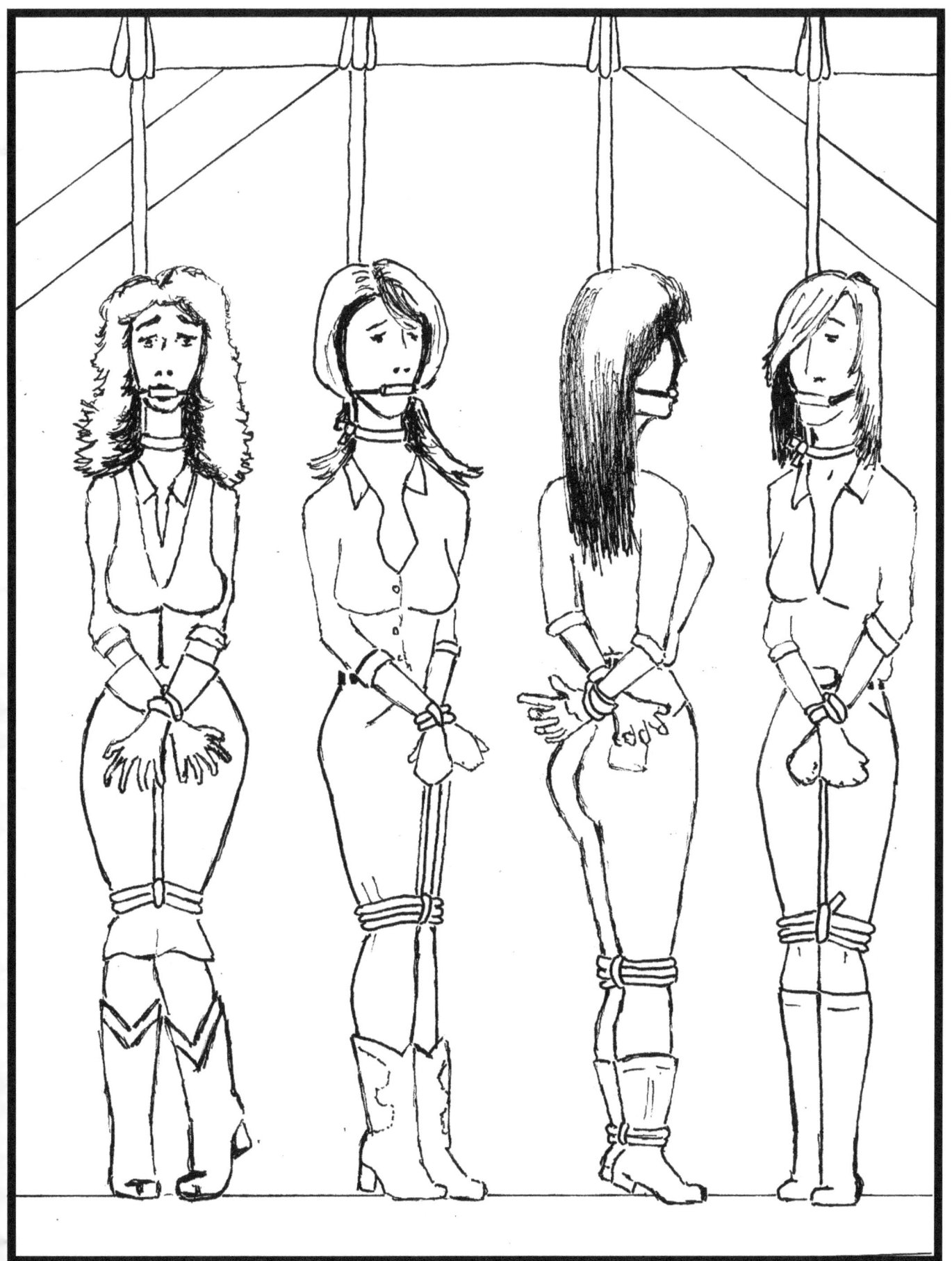

TIFFANY, DAPHNE, HEATHER & FAITH ANN HELD IN THE HOLD OF THE YACHT
IN THE ROCKABILLY CAPER

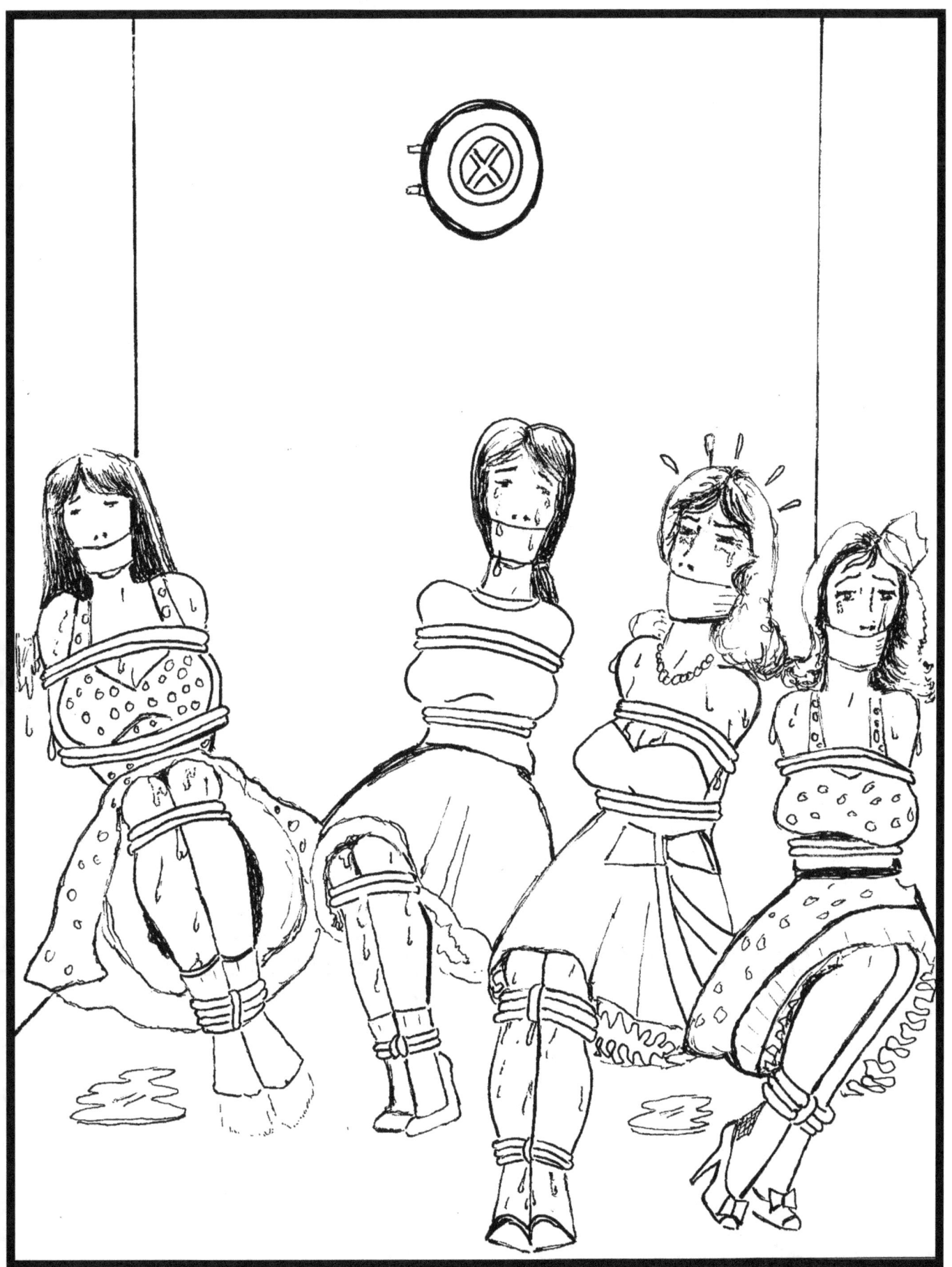

KESLEY STRAPPED TO THE TABLE • IN THE GIRLS COLLEGE CAPER
BOOK COVER

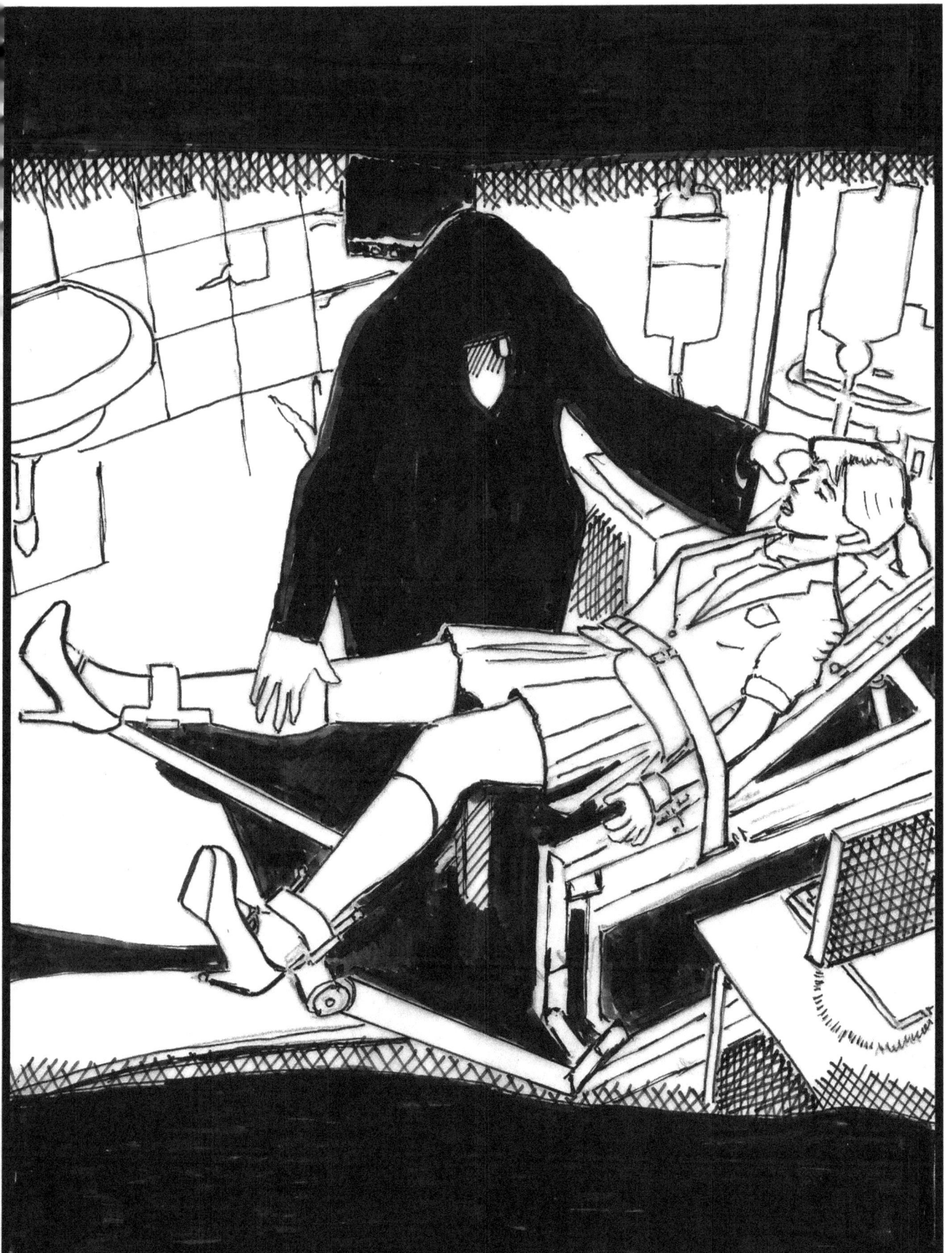

FIONE, ABOUT TO BE GAGGED WITH HER OWN SOCK
IN THE BEAUTY CONTEST CAPER

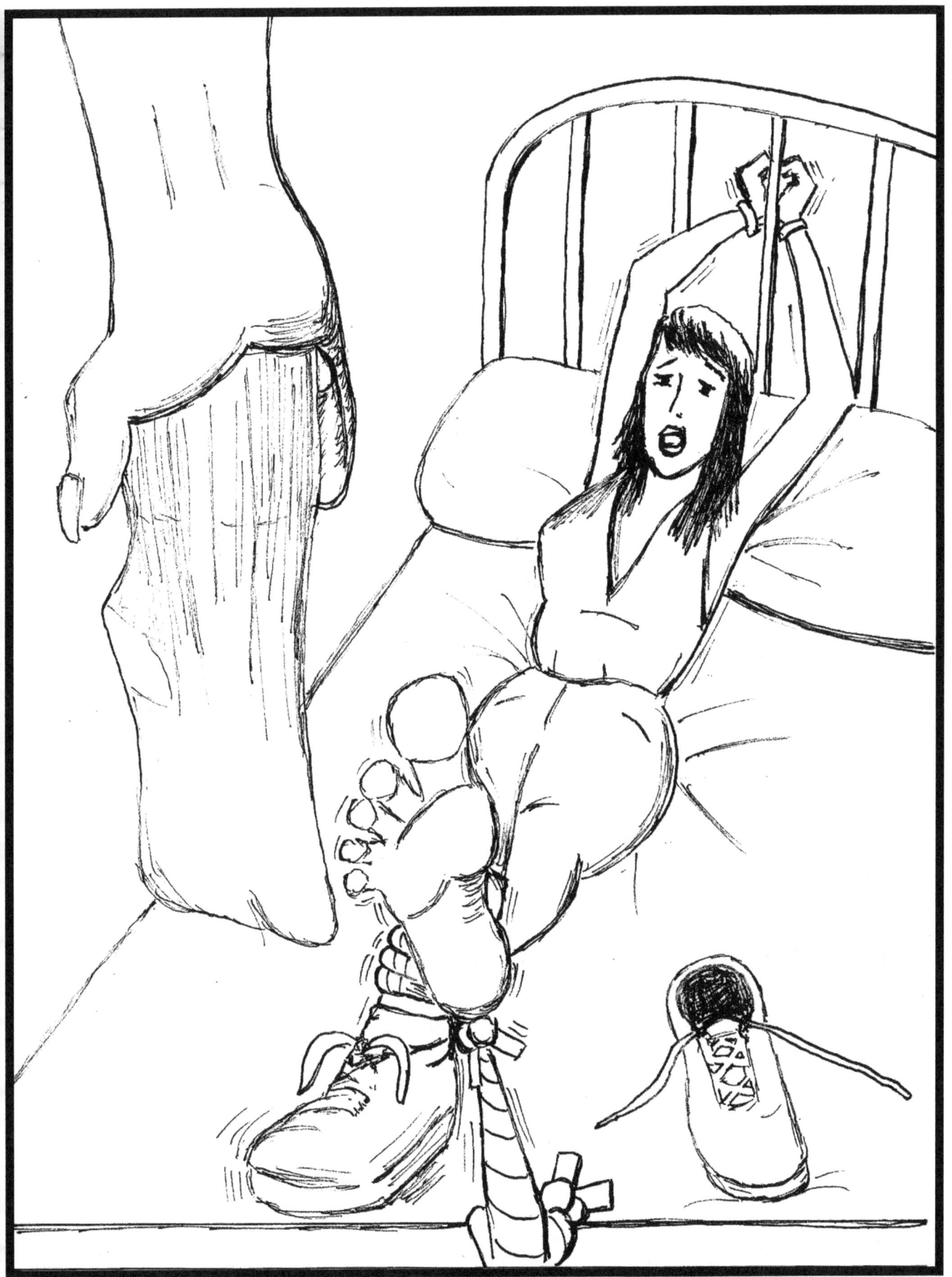

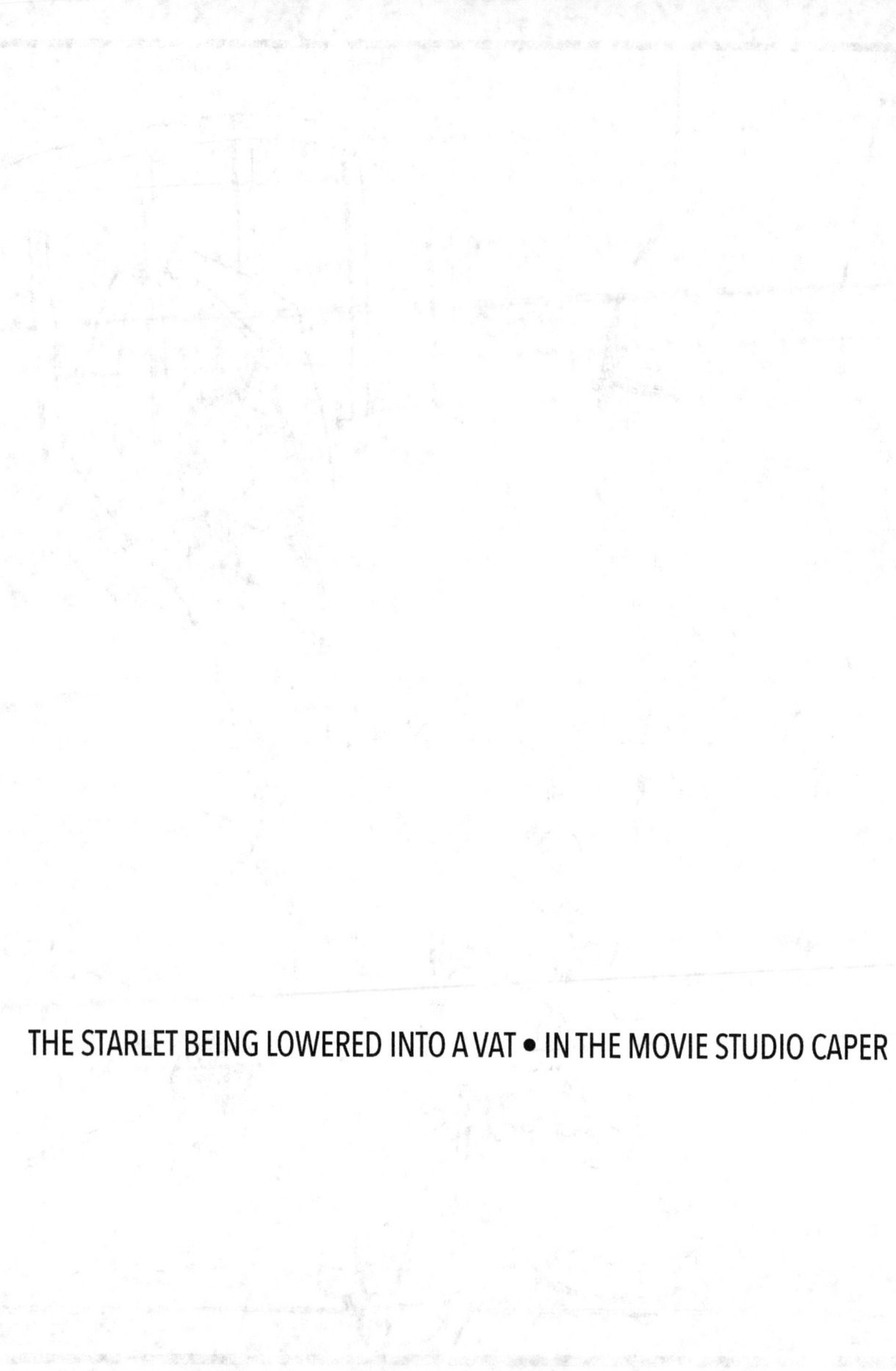

THE STARLET BEING LOWERED INTO A VAT • IN THE MOVIE STUDIO CAPER

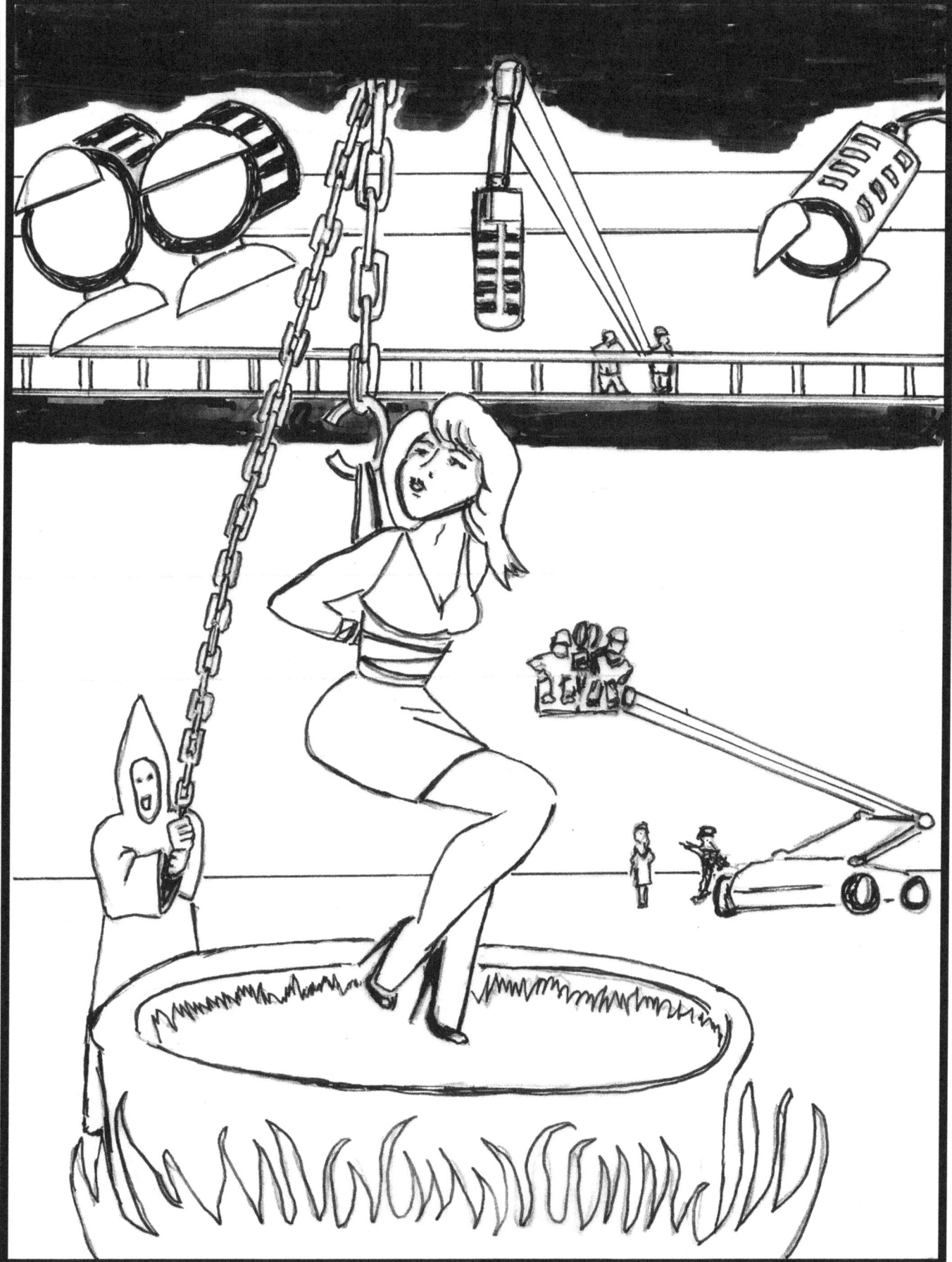

PHYLLIS AND HER DAUGHTERS, ERICA AND CINDY BEING CAPTURED
IN 'HOME INVASION'
BOOK COVER

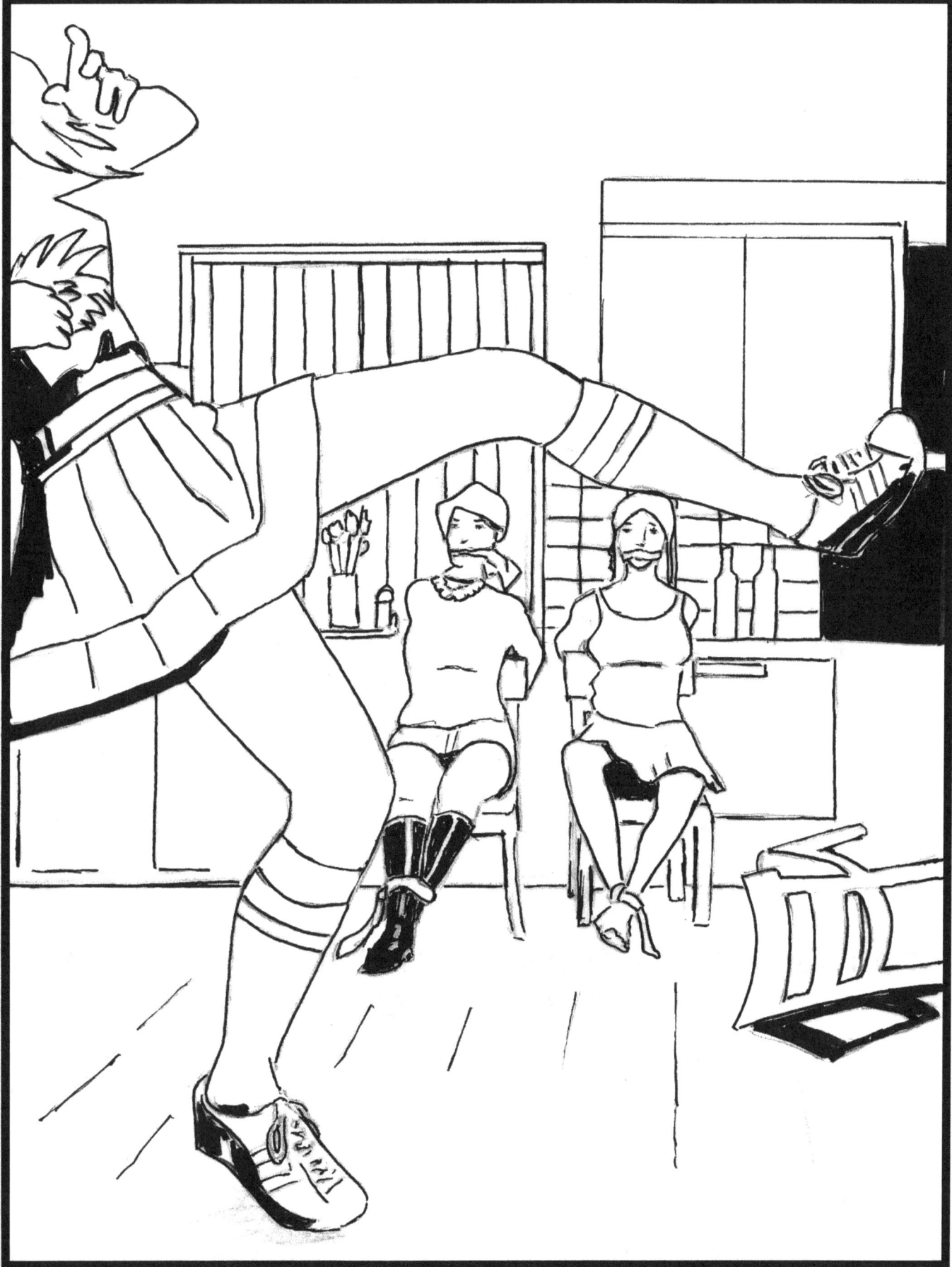

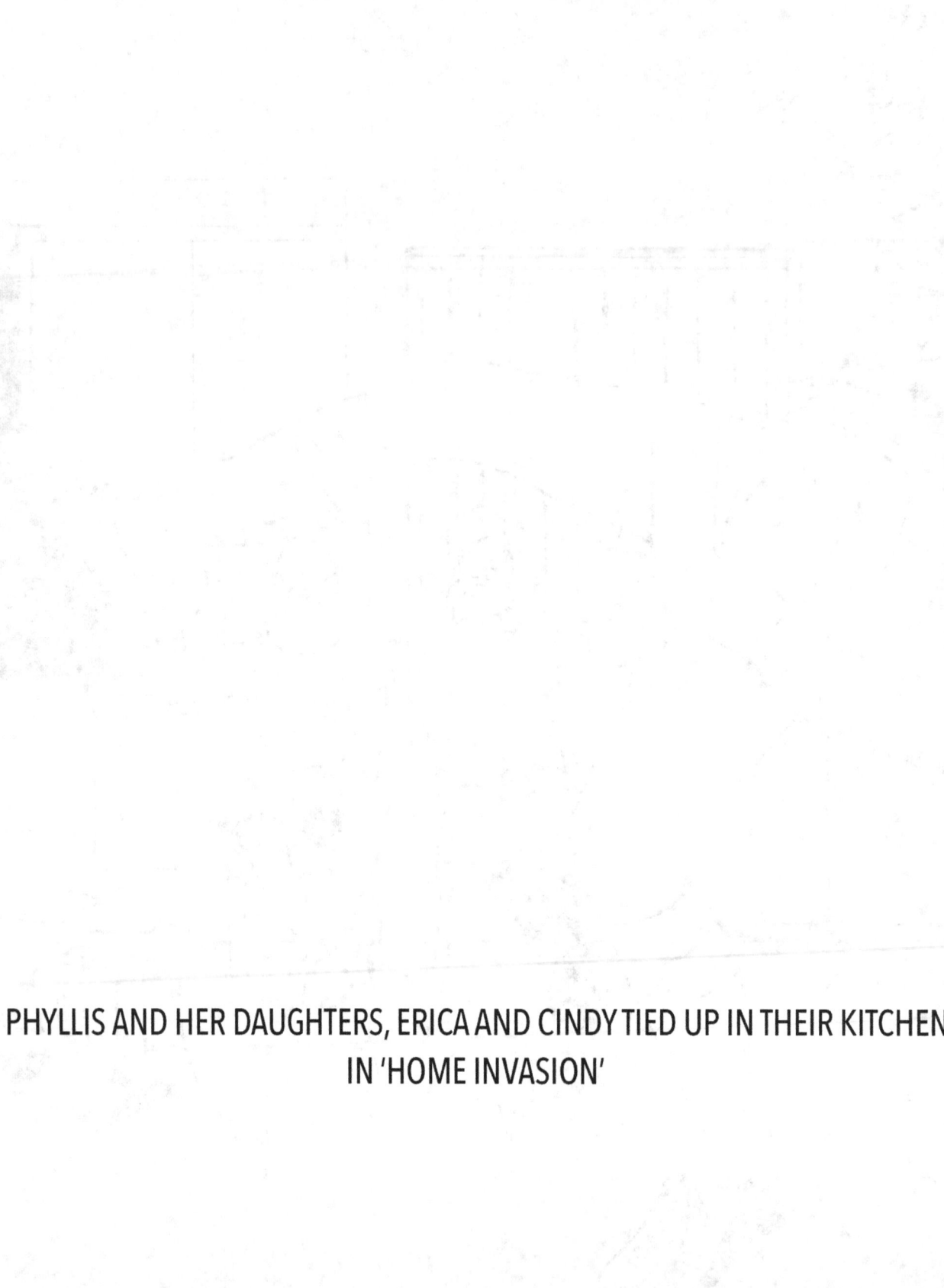

PHYLLIS AND HER DAUGHTERS, ERICA AND CINDY TIED UP IN THEIR KITCHEN IN 'HOME INVASION'

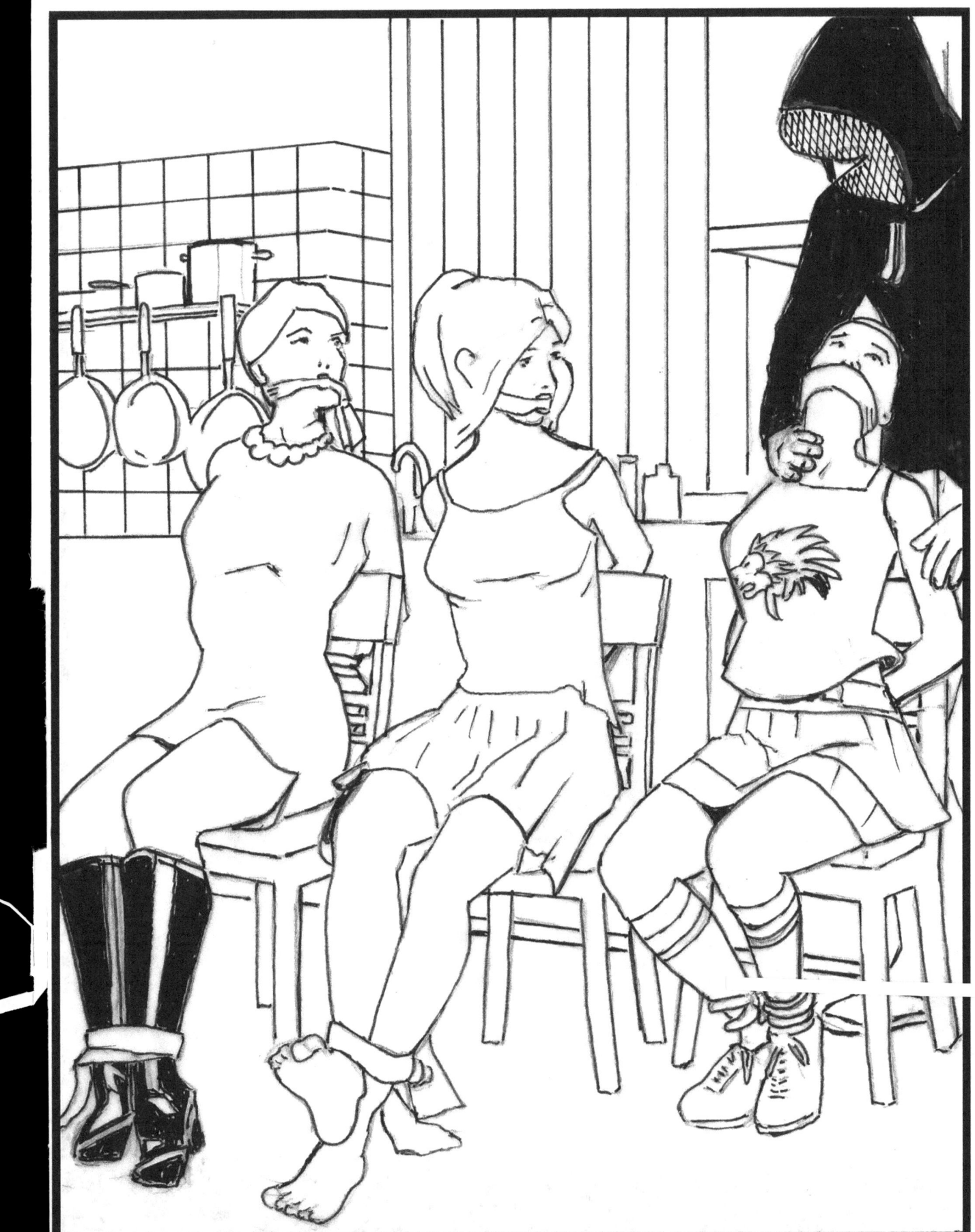

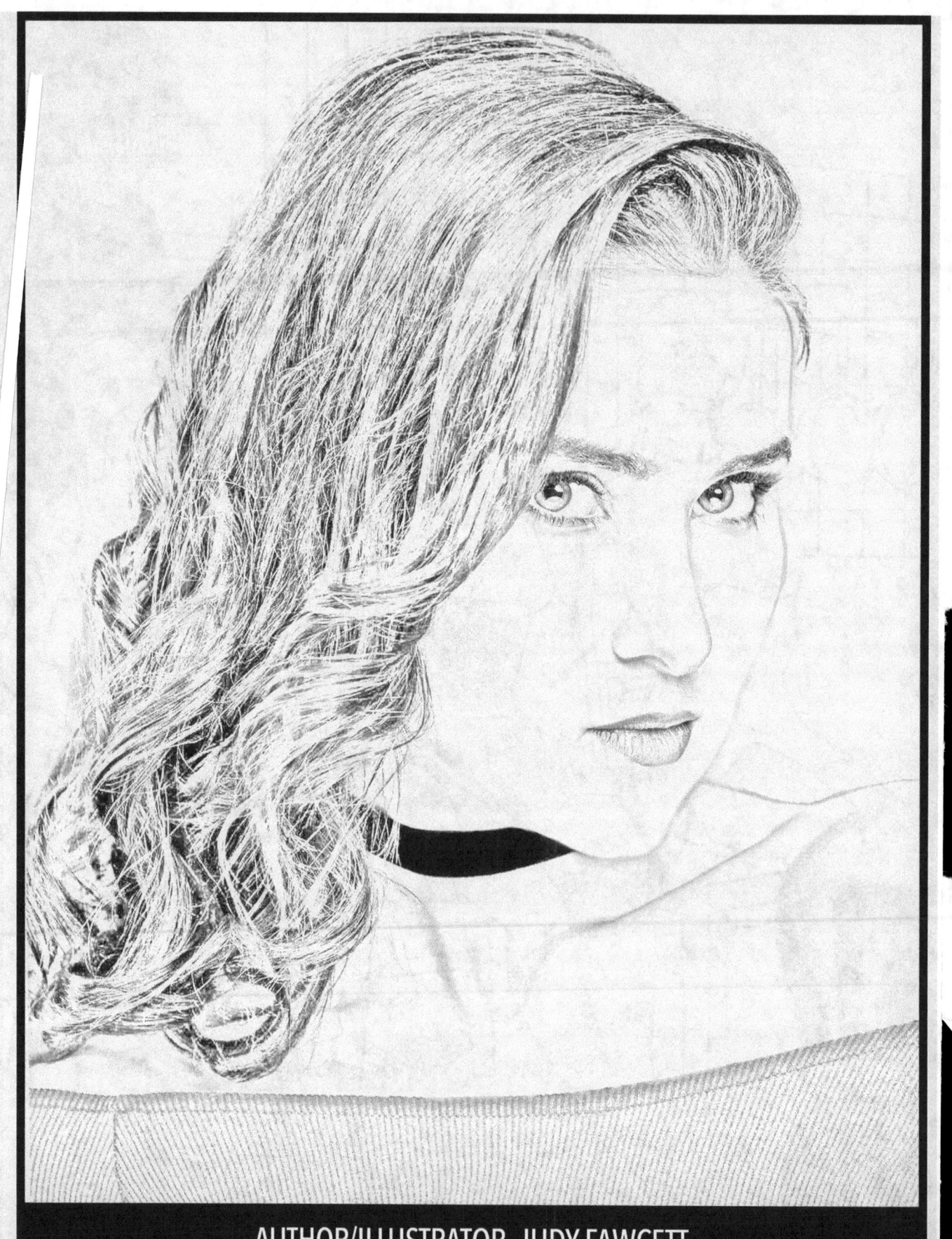

AUTHOR/ILLUSTRATOR, JUDY FAWCETT

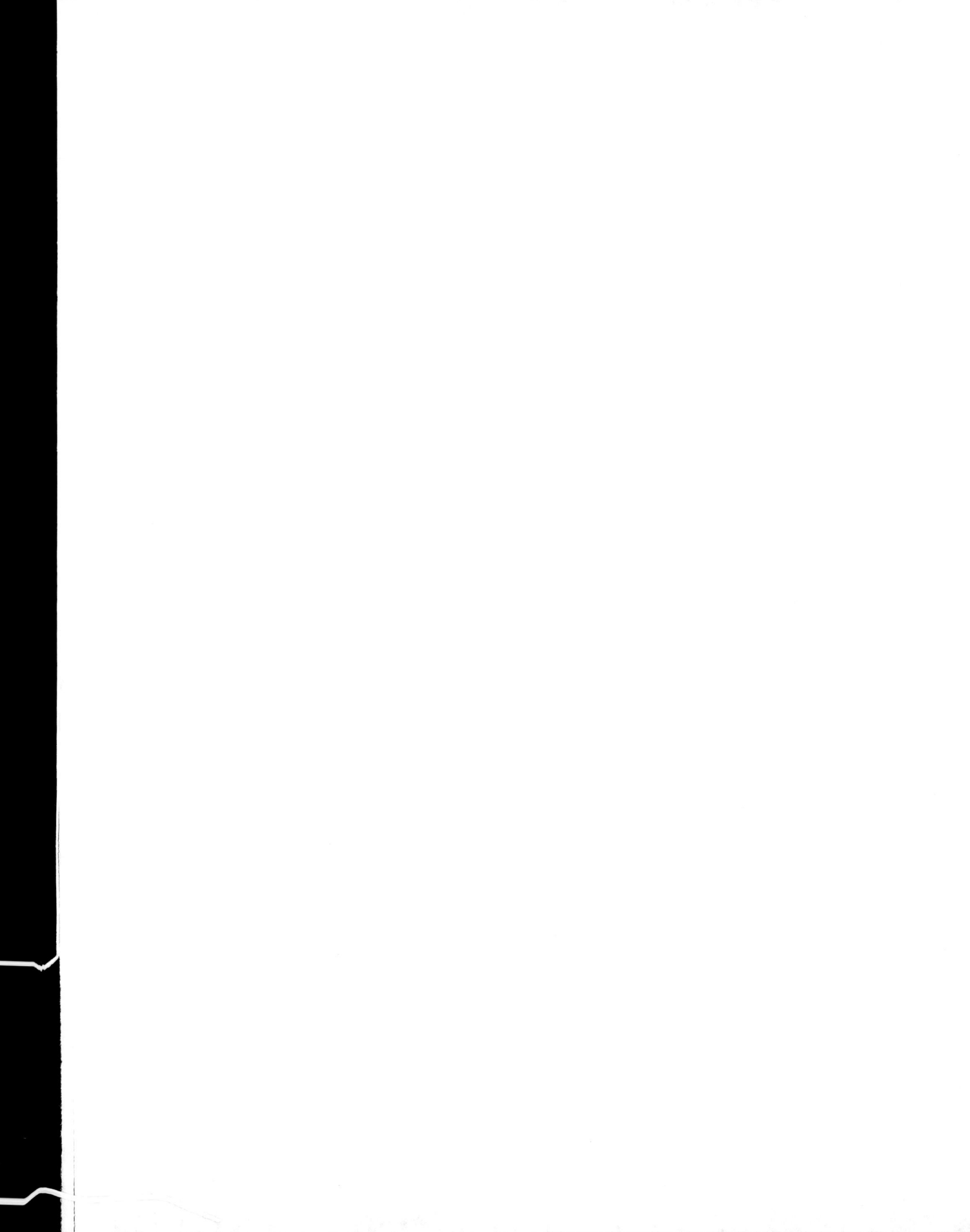

www.ingramcontent.com/pod-product-compliance
Lightning Source LLC
Chambersburg PA
CBHW080441220526
45465CB00007B/2/21